HAUNTED
SUMTER COUNTY,
FLORIDA

HAUNTED
SUMTER COUNTY,
FLORIDA

DEBORAH CARR HOLLINGSWORTH

FOREWORD BY JANICE OBERDING

HAUNTED
America

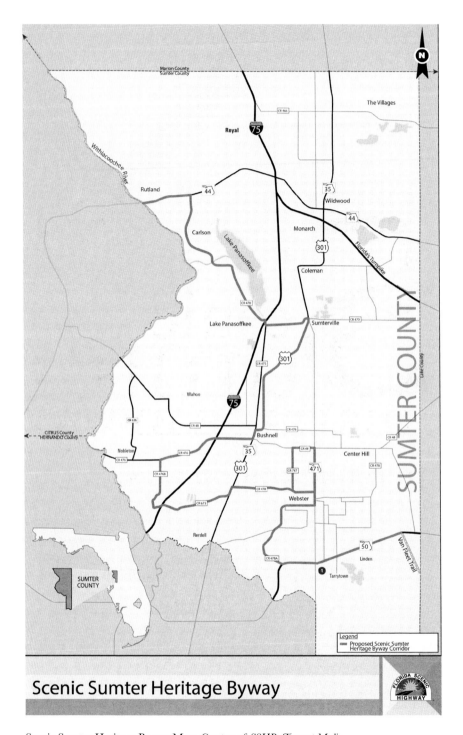

Scenic Sumter Heritage Byway Map. *Courtesy of SSHB–Tangent Media.*

Scenic Sumter Heritage Byway Logo. *Courtesy of SSHB–Tangent Media.*

Published by Haunted America
A Division of The History Press
Charleston, SC
www.historypress.com

Copyright © 2019 by Deborah Carr Hollingsworth
All rights reserved

First published 2019

Manufactured in the United States

ISBN 9781467144209

Library of Congress Control Number: 2019943521

Notice: The information in this book is true and complete to the best of our knowledge. It is offered without guarantee on the part of the author or The History Press. The author and The History Press disclaim all liability in connection with the use of this book.

Dedicated to…

My mom, Alfa Faye Watson Carr (1932–2019). Her dream became my dream.

My dad, Garnard "Gary" Tann Carr. A living testament that hard work does pay off.

My husband, Dr. Larry L. Hollingsworth. His Native American heart beats within my own.

CONTENTS

FOREWORD

Florida's Sumter County may not be large as far as counties go, but covering its rich and diverse history and its ghosts was certainly a formidable task. After reading this book, it's clear that Deborah Carr Hollingsworth was up to the challenge. But then again, I didn't doubt it for a moment. Deborah is my friend. And I do not use the words *my friend* lightly. Deborah (Deb) and I have been friends for many, many years. In those years, I have come to admire her enthusiasm and diligence in leaving no stone unturned when it comes to digging up historical information or finding answers for a haunting. I have also come to believe that she is an especially gifted medium.

I've known this since the first day I met her in Virginia City, Nevada, way back in the day. This was a time before ghost investigators were considered normal, before paranormal TV was all the rage, long before Zak Bagans, Jason Hawes and Grant Wilson became household names. So yes, it all began in Virginia City.

I was doing a ghost tour of Virginia City at the time. It happened that a woman with a delightful southern lilt called to make reservations for herself and her family. We chatted. And as we worked out the details, she informed me that she had always felt she was a medium. But, she explained, she didn't speak of this for fear of being made fun of in the small community she lived in. I ended our conversation by telling her, "We will see."

I gave several tours in the meantime, but the woman with the southern lilt and easy laughter stayed in my mind. Would she be as pleasant in person, I wondered? Or would she be, as my grandmother used to say, "A crackpot?"

I got my answer one bright day at the Silver Terrace Cemetery in Virginia City. I stepped from my vehicle to shake hands with a charming strawberry blonde who announced, "I'm Deborah and I can't wait to get started." I assess people quickly, and I knew: this woman was not a crackpot. I was immediately drawn to her. She seemed to be standing in two planes simultaneously: the earthly plane and the more ethereal plane where ghosts reside. That is how I perceive mediums. And that is how I saw Deb on that first meeting. She quickly introduced me to the other members of her group. Clearly, they didn't have the interest that she did. But they good-naturedly shook my hand and looked at the cemetery entrance. I'd seen that look before. And it said, "Let's go. The quicker we start, the quicker we will be finished."

They are just going to have to wait, I told myself. "So, Deborah, what do you feel?" I asked.

She smiled at me and then looked around and proceeded to astound me with what she was *picking up on.* Yes! She was the real deal! Many people don't realize that the Silver Terrace encompasses several different sections, but she did. Now keep in mind that this was long before anything but the most rudimentary of cellphones were in use, a time when everyone had AOL dialup and there wasn't a whole lot of information on the World Wide Web.

We walked past an area of the cemetery that faced mining tailings, and suddenly Deb stopped. "There's a little boy here. He's chasing his ball—he died here looking for the ball."

I'd heard the story before. But there was one part—one part I was waiting for.

"He has a sister here. She is older." Deb said.

I could have jumped with excitement. I hate to be wrong about people. Deb had just given me validation that she was indeed the real deal. And that I had been right in my original assessment of her. "You're the real deal!" I told her. "Few people see the sister, but you did."

As it turned out, I spent the afternoon with Deb discussing history and her gift and why she shouldn't let people throw shade on what is real and genuine. Deb, I was thrilled to realize, was not a one-trick pony. She was as interested in Virginia City's rich mining history as she was its ghostly inhabitants. At the end of the day I think we both realized that we were destined to be close friends.

Since our first meeting, we've traveled across the country and to Bermuda together, seeking ghosts and history. Deb is a people person. People are drawn to her kindness and warmth, both the living and the dead. Over the years, I've been amazed by some of the history she's been able to uncover using her mediumship abilities. And she continues to amaze me. There's her knack in finding unusual stories, the thorough historical research she puts into every project and of course the charisma that draws people to her as if she were a magnet. Deborah Carr Hollingsworth is a treasure to any community she chooses to reside in. Just as importantly, she is a treasure to any location she chooses to chronicle.

You, dear reader, are in for a treat. Deborah Carr Hollingsworth is a person whose *joie de vivre* shines through her writing. You're about to be pulled into all the historical, paranormal and unusual enchantment that is haunted Sumter County, Florida.

JANICE OBERDING
Author, Para-Celebrity, Historian

Warm sunlight dancing through the shady oaks on the backroads of Sumter County, Florida. *Courtesy of SSHB–Tangent Media.*

PREFACE

Interactive experiences abound within central Florida's Sumter County—from alligator encounters to wine tasting. An array of activities, sports and history is just outside your door. The Scenic Sumter Heritage Byway was first organized as a Community Action Group in 2009 and received its 501(c)3 in 2014. The Byway vision is to promote and protect history, natural beauty and recreational potential for visitors, residents and future generations of Sumter County, Florida. The Byway invites everyone to "Spend a day in scenic Sumter County!"

And now, the supernatural offers an alternate traveler's guide to explore Sumter County. Swamp creatures, gangsters, UFOs, Bigfoot, spirits, ghosts, murder and a mystery or two—all await to tease and tests your sixth sense.

Imagine exploring on and off the Scenic Sumter Heritage Byway in Sumter County, Florida, not by using a road map or GPS for directions but rather your own intuition for the destination.

Skeptic or believer, the supernatural unravels an alternate adventure in Sumter County, Florida.

From left to right: Baker House volunteers Beth Crouch-Payne, Linda Anderson, Larry and Laurie Bailey, the author, Cheryl Trask, Tanya Mikeals and Esther Bulger at Victorian Tea. *Courtesy of Crouch-Payne and Mikeals' collection.*

The SSHB team: Doug Smiley, Dan McCormick, Claudia Calzaretta (FDOT), Martin Steele and Christy Smiley. *Courtesy of SSHB–Tangent Media.*

ACKNOWLEDGEMENTS

Thank you to everyone who continues to share their own stories of the past so we may know what lies in the future.

A special thank-you to the Baker House docents and volunteers and to the Scenic Sumter Heritage Byway committee for their amazing gifts and foresights to keep the spirit of Sumter County's residents, past and present alive for the future generations!

Disclaimer: Sumter County, Florida's historic past is vastly diverse. Using an amazing amount of resources, local accounts and stories, I have done my best to piece together and present the area's past with respect and homage to what others experienced before me and will experience after me.

INTRODUCTION

Never did I think I was going to end up in central Florida. "Too flat, too humid and too hot" was often my reply to the idea of living in the sunshine state of Florida.

My parents, Alfa and Gary Carr, had lived in The Villages, Florida, since 2000. They enjoyed their enchanted lifestyle. By January 2017, my mom's health had declined. I knew that living near them was going to be a necessity. My own private life was being pulled in many directions. Then fate stepped in.

Later that winter, I was driving from my parents' Villages home to the Tampa Airport to pick up my boyfriend (now husband), Larry. It was a gorgeous winter's day, sunny and in the seventies—a beautiful day for a drive and an unexpected paranormal experience. Road construction detoured me off the main highway just as my phone rang. I pulled over to answer, looked around and realized that I was in the middle of an old cemetery. As I finished my conversation, the energy around me shifted. I was being lifted, and my physical being floated beyond the moment. The spirits floated out of their graves and greeted me.

I'm not sure exactly what the spirits said. I just remember that feeling of clarity. I was deep in the heart of sunny Florida while most of the United States was blanketed with snow. Just like all the other pioneers before me—Native Americans, European explorers, African Americans, settlers, soldiers, ranchers and retirees—I knew I belonged here. The weather melted my heart, and the soul of Florida spoke to me. My own personal journey into historic and haunted Sumter County, Florida, began that day.

I do believe that Florida has a way of drawing you in. Just as with all the generations before me, the land haunts me with its huge magical oaks, rich vegetation, cool waters and a history hidden deep inside each Florida's resident's heart…past, present and future.

SUMTER COUNTY: A BRIEF HISTORY

More than twelve thousand years ago, the glaciers moved across the North American continent, and nearly ten thousand years back, the aboriginal tribes found their way to Florida. The land was abundant with wildlife, waterways and idealistic climates to adequately provide for the thriving early residents for many generations until the unexpected arrival of outsiders.

The unforeseen appearances of Spaniards and other explorers began in the late 1400s and early 1500s. These foreigners were deadly to the original tribes. Sadly, by the early 1700s, European colonists had wiped out most of the early natives and their culture by murder, disease and slavery.

Some of the deserted, sacred Indian land was eventually resettled by other tribes who often intermarried with the remaining "wild" local clans and "runaway" slaves to create what Spaniards coined the "Seminole people." Foreign settlers were soon joined by domestic pioneers from other states and territories in the United States, including South and North

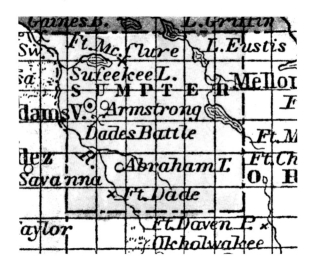

Historic Sumter County Map, 1856. *Courtesy of FCIT.*

Carolina, Virginia, Alabama, Tennessee, Kentucky and Georgia. A variety of cultures and the need for land continues to threaten the survival of all of Florida's residents.

The official possession of Florida was shifted between several foreign countries until the United States successfully purchased Florida from Spain in 1821. On March 3, 1845, Florida, the twenty-seventh state, entered the union. Meanwhile, the Seminole Wars (1817–58) battled on between Florida's Seminoles, foreign bodies, new settlers and the U.S. government. The Florida war was the longest, costliest and bloodiest Indian war in United States history. Eventually, 250 to 300 of the surviving Seminoles scattered throughout southern Florida. The others, not killed, were forced to travel the Trail of Tears to what is now Oklahoma.

Since then, the faces and cultures of Florida's people have evolved among these fertile lands. Change continues to alter the fate of Sumter County's residents. Highways, interstates and attractions, along with retirement communities, coexist among the homesteaders, ranchers, old battlefields, ghost towns and graveyards of the past. The populations may have shifted, but the land remains constant, haunted with the history of the past.

Intuitively, is it possible to encounter the many historical struggles of central Florida's societies? While you sit among hidden graveyards, walk battlefields and step among the ruins of real ghost towns, the heart and soul of Sumter County will speak. It is the land that is haunted. Mysteries still await to be uncovered, and the night sky lights the way to encourage all seekers of the truth on this pilgrimage of historic and haunted Sumter County, Florida.

PART I

BACKROAD BLUNDERS AND DISCOVERIES

OFF THE BYWAY

I kept hearing the crying…

UPPER SUMTER COUNTY HISTORY BRIEFING

Years before the War Between the States, white settlers and freed and runaway slaves, among others, were entering central Florida to create new lives amid the indigenous people. The Native American way of life was continuously challenged by the invasion of alternate cultures.

The upper region of what is now Sumter County provided land and business opportunities for the incoming outsiders. This area was soon formally established. One such community was known as Long Hammock. According to Hulon H. Nichols's book *Long Hammock Memories*, "There has never been much history written about it or the entire northwest part of Sumter County. The reason being, old families listed in this book have basically kept our mouths shut, lived quiet lives and worked very hard, sometimes just to survive." Quite a testament considering that's what most want—a peaceful way of life. Living is hard enough.

Intuitively, this region carries an ancient, peaceful energy of its own. Despite past and future conflicts, the different cultures in this area, according to what was recorded, seemed to live in productive harmony.

In the very early 1800s, white settlers established their businesses and homes in what is now the northern end of Sumter County. Nearby, free slaves and perhaps a few runaways had located in and near what is now named Royal, and together these early families began milling operations and cloth weaving. The area's Seminoles, some say, were considered allies. Long ago, some Seminoles had established their own villages, and others chose a nomadic lifestyle. Harmonious respect was needed for each culture to survive in the wilds of Florida. Traces of these past cultures may still be uncovered among the local communities and cemeteries. Haunted history offers an alternate way to hear of each culture's struggle and triumphs.

OAK GROVE CEMETERY, WILDWOOD

It was a typical beautiful sunny Florida's winter afternoon when I decided to try to find Royal on my own. Royal is one of Florida's oldest existing African American communities. I admit that my mind was a bit scattered. The book's writing lacked direction. Yet I was passionate to see what I could find in Royal. Off I went driving down the county roads as the GPS instructed, heading toward Royal from my lake home in Fruitland Park. Deeper and deeper into the wild woods I journeyed. Just as I turned a sharp corner, there was an old wooden sign, clearly pointing me toward Oak Grove Cemetery. Deep inside, I knew that my course of direction had changed, at least temporarily. After following a few well-guided wooden signs, I drove right up to Oak Grove Cemetery. I quickly hopped out, gave my ritual prayer of honor and respect for the residents and then paused to wonder, "Why was I sent here?"

Ancient and modern monuments were tucked neatly among the heavily draped trees. A covered shelter clearly divided the cemetery. Intuitively, I was drawn to the backend of the graveyard. There among the stones and bushes was a box turtle. He was at least twelve inches across, his neck stuck out, and without blinking he gazed directly into my eyes. I was clearly losing this staring contest. For a minute there, I thought about taking him home, but I knew better. And then the meaning hit me right between the eyes. The turtle was exactly where he belonged, and I had found him!

My mind rushed back to the past. Several years ago, a midwestern Native American craftsman named Dell had made me a ceremonial drum and by his own selection picked the turtle as my spirit animal. I admit that at the time, I wasn't too thrilled. Why not a hawk? Or a snake? My chosen spirit didn't seem quite so romantic. But the meaning is my truth now, just like it was when Dell chose it for me. According to Native American beliefs, the turtle represents Mother Earth, being grounded and patient—attributes, clearly, I had been lacking lately.

I gazed at that turtle for quite some time. Accepting and recognizing my truth, I knew I was where I needed to be. There were stories to be told. It was essential for me to slow down and pace myself. By doing so, I could take the necessary steps, with confidence, to allow haunted Sumter County, Florida stories to come alive! Yes, my animal spirit guide was there, and I was listening. This would be the beginning of many mysteries later found at Oak Grove Cemetery.

As I was leaving, I turned back. I was being led to revisit a particular site. Earlier, I had noticed that it was an old aboveground crypt. It is common in some lowland areas to place a loved one inside such a receptacle. This allows the decaying body to stay intact and not float out of the ground. This aged crypt appeared to have tightly molded itself around the actual shape of the contained body. I bent down, touched the area of the heart and felt an instant kinetic kinship with the resident and the land. Once again, the haunted land spoke to me.

The turtle is often associated with one's physical and embodied evolution on the earthly plane. Intuitively, my heart experienced a deeper yearning and connection to many mysteries at Oak Grove Cemetery. But it was my dearly departed friend John Reardon Scott, who died on March 8, 1900, who connected me, that day, with historic Sumter County, Florida.

Raised crypt, Oak Grove Cemetery. *Author's collection.*

THE PEOPLE OF ROYAL

Her name is "T." She is a direct descendant of one of Royal's original citizens. I just happened to meet her by chance after I left Oak Grove Cemetery. I was following the road out of the cemetery to reach Florida's historic marker for the Royal School Site. As I pulled into the parking lot, I noticed a small yard/food sale was set up right across from the state marker. I scanned the state marker and felt privileged to stand among such a remarkable African American community.

My thoughts then turned back to the local vendor tables. One young man was selling some homemade goodies. He was eager to explain how his family recipes came to be. His grandpa still made syrup and sweets from Royal land. The generations of sugar cane and the people living on the land provided some sweet goodness, served with kindness.

T's booth was nearby, I noticed her wide variety of colorful shoes, clothes and handbags. I walked over, admiring her items, and then we got to talking. She explained how she lived on her grandfather's original forty acres along with other relatives. She spoke of her grandfather and how he and a few other African American families had settled here shortly after the Civil War. She was born and raised in the area, prospered in Philadelphia, New York and Miami and returned home "after her kids were educated and grown." She said, "This is where I belong."

Her grandfather had been buried on the property, and as we reminisced about home, land and family, I felt an overwhelming kinship to this woman. As I made my purchases and left, I felt a shift within me, to the left of my heart. I was feeling blessed by sharing in her story of her family in Royal. I felt then what I read about later, that such a peaceful coexistence occurred in the early years of the area. She also informed me that usually on the first Saturday of the month, a history tour is given at the Royal School Site. I plan to return—besides, the cane sugar goodies were worth the trip, as was my new friendship with T.

Before the official naming of Royal, several African American families had already quietly settled in the area during the early 1800s. It was known as Royalville. Indeed, history has proven that the early residents were kin to African royalty.

After the war, freed slaves, including those from the nearby Old Green Plantation located on the Withlacoochee River, were awarded forty acres by President Lincoln's executive order. As landowners, this would help them to establish themselves as free citizens of the United States. Even though the original directive did not technically include a mule, some residents were indeed given an old army mule.

Officially founded in 1865, Royal was originally named Picketsville. Each landowner took great pride in building a white picket fence completely around the cabin area. A clear view of the homestead's yard could warn the family of any unwelcome guests. The interior of the yard enclosure was cleared of debris, including trees and brush. The pretty white picket fence kept wild hogs and loose cattle at bay. The open field reinforced the family's safety. If a rattler or other unwanted ground rodent approached, it could be killed and swept away from the dwelling. After President Abraham Lincoln's assassination, the original order was rescinded by the new president, Andrew Johnson. Luckily, Royal residents were firmly established in their homesteads, and many descendants, such as T, still reside there today.

In July 2011, the Royal Church celebrated its 136th year. As reported in the *Sumter County Times*, "On Sunday, July 17, Ebenezer African Methodist Episcopal Church, Royal celebrated, providing spiritual uplifting, comfort and services to the Community of Royal."

I believe that anyone entering the community will recognize what I felt—a freedom and peace that is rare and often short-lived in most communities.

OXFORD, INCLUDING PINE LEVEL CEMETERY

I kept hearing the crying as I entered the Nichols Cemetery. Where was I being led?...Let's slow down the story and take a few steps back into the past.

It all began earlier that Sunday morning. As I was waking up, I heard a weak cry. Was it a bird or a small animal outside my window, or perhaps a spirit reaching out from the beyond? Anything was possible. I knew that someone or something was in distress. I had to get up, get going and find out what was going on.

I asked Larry right away if he was willing to drive and help me find some sites for the book. He didn't know about the crying though. The plan was to revisit the town of Oxford; its cemetery, Pine Level; and the nearby Nichols Cemetery in Long Hammock. These historic sites were tucked down a few scenic backcountry roads just beyond The Villages retirement community and before Interstate 75.

Larry drove around the Oxford community a few times as I recorded my psychic impressions. Oxford, according to the old-timers, was sparsely settled among a pine forest in 1840. In 1850, the only town in Sumter County, Florida, was Adamsville, ten miles south. Oxford was originally called Sandspur and is the second-oldest town in Sumter County. It was once an ample community with a bustling hotel, post office and one of the largest student bodies at the local public school.

In those days, most settlers raised corn, cotton, peanuts, hogs and cattle. The mail was originally delivered by stagecoach. When the railroad came into town, to avoid confusion with similar terminal stops, the town was renamed Oxford. There are two known stories about the municipality's new name. B.F. Borden, one of the locals, suggested renaming the town after his original hometown of Oxford, Alabama. Others claimed that an alternate play on words lead to the new designation. The story goes, that the pond right outside the town's four-corner stop would often flood over the main road during heavy rains. The mud and muck would cause major road havoc. Traveling pioneers and supply wagons were known to get completely stuck. This required the assistance of a local ox team to ford them out of the unwelcome sludge. Either way, the name Oxford stuck.

Nearby, the present busy route of Highway 301 was once known as "Jackson's Trail." After serving in the War of 1812, General Andrew Jackson invaded Florida in 1817 to represent the U.S. government in the deadly Seminole Wars. He created Jackson's Trail as part of his plan to remove the Seminoles and recapture runaway black slaves. Over a twelve-year period, Jackson served as a general, U.S. senator and the president of the United States; at the same time, three major bloody conflicts, political negotiations, skirmishes and unfulfilled promises eventually led to the forced eradication of most of the remaining Seminoles in 1835. Their physical bodies may have followed Jackson's route on the Trail of Tears, but spiritually, the Seminole soul still lives on throughout Florida and Sumter County.

Very little is left of the old buildings in Oxford, and the town's residences are scattered among deeply wooded foliage. Some say, to this day, that the busy cross section remains haunted. After a heavy rain, when the mist hangs low in the trees, you can still hear the faint sound of a cracking whip, snorting oxen and creaking wagons.

Jackson's Trail is now bustling Highway 301, a major artery from Oxford's settlement back into civilization. The haunted Seminole legends are also revealed in other regions of the Scenic Sumter Heritage Byway.

It's, well, a mystery. *Author's collection.*

The weeping began again, and my mind drifted to the next destination. Will Pine Level Cemetery afford any answers to the psychic cry? The cemetery was easily located down a few backroads, off the main highway. The Oxford Cemetery Association was incorporated in May 1888 and still maintains and operates this beautiful country cemetery—a peaceful setting among the old oaks that eternally marks the passing of many early settlers and their descendants.

Through the cemetery organization's write-up, I had read about and wanted to locate the old sundial piece. After disembarking from the truck, I found the monument right away. I watched, fascinated, as the play of light and shade danced across the face of time. A moment of time is time well spent.

My attention was then given to a nearby oddity: a stone wishing well. The circular base consisted of cemented stacked stones. Its foundation supported a well-chiseled rocked archway. The well was my size, not too tall. I could have easily drawn water up from the well or cast a wish.

Baffled by its use, I looked around for any clues. No headstone or plaque gave reference to this interesting icon. I was delighted by the piece because I didn't have to stand on my tiptoes to look inside.

The well had me guessing. Later inquiries of its purpose were divided among the locals. A planter, a wishing well, a giant Easter egg basket or a displaced cattle trough were just a few of the guesses. And then I heard the cry again. This time it was distant. Outside the cemetery.

The unusual well, despite my wishes, remains a small mystery. And the sobbing soul, apparently, was not inside Pinewood Level Cemetery. I realized it was time to move on. After my parting prayers, I headed back to the truck. Was this remorseful wail guiding me to the Nichols Cemetery?

NICHOLS FAMILY CEMETERY, LONG HAMMOCK

The Nichols Cemetery was only a few miles away. My own mind was still ticking away to locate the source of the weeping. The backcountry road's beauty soothed the energy all around us. The huge oaks and pines managed to block most of the interstate noise as we entered the cemetery.

In 1880, the Nichols Family Cemetery was established by William Robert "Bob" Nichols Sr. The Nichols Cemetery Association Inc. was

Eternal mother-and-child reunion at Nichols Family Cemetery. *Author's collection.*

established on October 15, 1979. The family continues to prosper, and the association provides a tranquil final resting place for many generations to come.

Founder Bob, according to local history, was one of the first permanent residents at Nichols Cemetery. He lies exactly seven feet south of his "Talk Tree." Depending on one's beliefs, a Talk Tree manifests the ability to talk and protect and communicate with the plant and animal kingdom, as well as humankind.

Bob probably used his own Talk Tree to stay grounded and guided in time of need. Scientists now believe that there is a kernel of truth to the mystical ancient Talk Tree legend, given a tree's uncanny ability to commune with other life forms. Many believe that Talk Trees can relay information through the air, using pheromones and other scent signals to communicate to another life form's basic senses. They can protect, predict and provide for the willing recipients. Next time you hug a tree, hear rustling leaves or witness bark crack and fall, take the time and ask the tree, "What are you trying to tell me?" You might be surprised by the answers.

As Larry and I arrived at the fenced Nichols Cemetery, I heard the weeping again. I looked around for something or someone to help me. It was louder this time. Frantic now, I jumped out of the truck and started to run from grave to grave. I grabbed at trees, steadying myself as I bent down to quickly scan dates and names on the headstones.

I wasn't sure what or whom I was looking for as the sobbing continued. As I covered the entire cemetery area, I noticed that there were many graves of young children that dated as far back as the 1800s to the present. Some lived a day or two, others for several years. Perhaps this was the sound of a grieving mother or a lost child? I stopped in my tracks, braced my back against the nearest tree and slowly slid down the tree with tears in my eyes. And the weeping ceased. There was a dead hush.

A heavy weight rose from my beating heart. I immediately bowed my head in silence. I slowly made my way back to the truck with a lighter and more gracious heart. I had recently lost my own mother to dementia, and at that moment, I was humbly reminded of the eternal mother-and-child reunion that lives beyond the grave. Being a family cemetery, perhaps the residents were reaching through time to find a way to comfort me in my time of grief? Because that is what family does. It was a powerful message of eternal love.

After leaving the Nichols Cemetery, I thought I would never experience that cry again, and yet the past finds a way to speak. The haunted road off the Scenic Sumter Heritage Byway leads right into a very civilized retirement community.

THE VILLAGES

Just a few roads away from Sumter County's rural past is the prospering presence of The Villages. Interwoven among the tri-counties of Sumter, Lake and Marion, the modern-day Disney World of retirement communities continues to thrive. But even modern dreams have an intriguing heritage.

Years back, Harold Schwartz had a dream. As a Michigan businessman, he was selling a "piece of paradise" via mail order, enticing future retirees to move to the lands of endless sunshine and relaxation. Schwartz sold land in Florida and New Mexico on the installment plan. According to Inside the Bubble (https://www.insidethebubble.net), one could buy the future with ten dollars down and ten dollars per month—a highly affordable dream to any everyday Joe.

By the 1960s, many retirement communities such as Del Webb's in Sun City in Tampa were flourishing. However, with the dream came the realization that perhaps some of those earlier "sight unseen" land purchases were swampland. Many retirees pressured the government to protect their investments, and in 1968, Congress banned land sales by mail. "Seeing was believing."

Spanish Springs Town Square, The Villages. *Courtesy of Larry Hollingsworth.*

34

In the early 1970s, Schwartz and his partner, Al Tarrson, revamped their Florida real estate business and built a mobile home park called Orange Blossom Gardens. It was ideally located in northwest Lake County right in the middle of a cow pasture. The dream was difficult to sell in such a rural setting. By the early 1980s, only four hundred homes had been sold. Schwartz was determined to create the utopia he had envisioned many years before.

Schwartz bought out Tarrson and brought aboard his son and daughter-in-law, Gary and Sharon Morse. According to the official website (https://www.thevillages.com), together they planned, redesigned and founded the senior living concept of The Villages in Sumter County "with a vision to create a warm, secure and friendly hometown where all your retirement dreams come true."

The Villages is now one of the fastest-growing cities in the United States, currently covering more than 32.1 square miles (and growing) and reaping $1.5 billion in net worth from real estate development that began in the center of a cow pasture. Despite all the magical moments inside The Villages bubble, there are some supernatural occurrences that cannot be explained.

In the article "In The Villages: Where Supernatural Is Natural" from the August 1, 2016 edition of the *Lake & Sumter Style* magazine, it was noted that parapsychology, according to Ina Anderson and partner Bobbie Roberts, "is anything that falls outside the five senses."

Living within The Villages' luxurious dream, residents are offered the phenomenal opportunity to live beyond basic needs. The lifestyle here provides a parapsychological style of healthy living through endless activities and events that often parallel the paranormal. The Villages residents sometimes realize their own connection to the rituals of the paranormal. Many forms of the supernatural have thus been encountered and reported among the people here.

From the beginning of time, Bigfoot sightings have been recorded in many areas of the world. One such experience was recently investigated by the Bigfoot Field Researchers Organization (http://www.bfro.net) in The Villages. According to its website, BFRO was founded in 1995 and is "the only scientific research organization exploring the bigfoot/sasquatch mystery."

Research claims that such "wild men," or sasquatch, are drawn to easily obtainable water and vegetation sources. In addition to those needs, the warm, sunny climate in Sumter County, Florida, could certainly attract man or beast to The Villages.

In December 2012, as two partners were sitting outside, suddenly a loud cry pierced the still night. It was a noise they had never heard before. Familiar with the sounds made late in the day outside, the couple stated, "It wasn't a child's cry or a coyote's wail." Completely baffled, one asked the other, "Is that Bigfoot?" The strange noise didn't repeat that night.

The following night, while sitting alone outside, one of the residents heard the distinct sound of two rocks being clacked together. The noise seemed to come from the back of the property. No other unusual sound was heard that evening.

The mystery continued a few nights later. For two consecutive evenings, an unknown odor permeated the air. Not foul, just not recognizable. The residents' dog deeply sniffed the smell but, oddly, did not react.

Another unusual occurrence happened a few nights later. Pebbles were being thrown by something or someone against the side of the house and lanai. At first it was just a few. A few nights later, the buildings were being attacked by a barrage of rocks. Bewildered, the owners pondered, "Could it be Bigfoot in the Villages?"

An inquiry was requested by the owners to BFO. Investigator R. Monteith reported and immediately noted, "The Villages, a master-planned age restricted retirement community in central Florida, is not your typical place for a sasquatch encounter." Nonetheless, as home to twenty-nine golf courses, this man-made environment could indeed provide the green areas and water needed to sustain any living creature.

The investigation revealed that the residents' house and property back up to a power line road that travels through The Villages, down rural avenues and then feeds directly into the Green Swamp—a perfect path for an uninvited creature. The investigator noted that the piercing sound could have been a bobcat or coyote. But the residents, familiar with such animal sounds, said it was "different."

The pebbles thrown were quite puzzling too until a similar sound was created with landscaped bark chips being thrown onto the home's aluminum siding.

The investigator walked beyond the property lines and discovered a large area that borders a golf course and the horse polo grounds, including the stables. While walking the back area, there appeared to be a ten-inch footprint in the earth. Just one. Both witnesses agreed that they had seen no one walk through that area, let alone barefooted. Not far away was a wild scat pile. Later research would report that no bear had been reported in the area for more than a year.

Investigator Monteith, highly educated and experienced in the crypto world, believes that this experience is not typical behavior of a sasquatch but that it is possible one could have followed the power line road down to The Villages.

Does Bigfoot roam Sumter County, Florida, or could there be an alternative supernatural explanation? Perhaps a local swamp or lake creature could be haunting the land? Bigfoot sightings are not typical in the Villages; however, night sky supernatural activities are superabundant.

The Villages lifestyle is often referred to as "Heaven here on Earth." How common are UFO sightings inside Sumter County's heavenly gates of The Villages? Are aliens trying to relocate? There are many ways to report, investigate and view UFO sightings and interactions with extraterrestrials. The number of reported sightings in Florida is astounding.

When living in the panhandle of Florida as children, my brother, Mike, and I shared a UFO sighting. Surprisingly, it was years later before each of us realized what we had independently experienced. I recalled the cigar-shaped objects, and he remembered the multiple colors emulating from the ships.

It was in the late '60s, while we were playing outside one evening, right before dark. The sky suddenly got very dark, and everything around us became very, very quiet. Even the birds quit singing. Stunned, we stood still, looked at each other and then looked up. A fleet of unidentified cigar-shaped objects was flying overhead. Multicolored lights flashed, and the supernatural ships disappeared as quickly as they had appeared.

The idea that aliens from another galaxy could be visiting Earth has fascinated Americans and the world for years. According to Don Johnson's online article "Here's How Florida Ranks for UFO Sightings" at Florida Patches (https://patch.com/florida), the Sunshine State, from 2001 to 2015, ranked second in the country for unidentified flying objects sightings with a total of 7,787 reported sightings during that time. Even though these recent numbers place Florida twenty-third overall, with the influx of The Villages reports, the recent sightings have increased with the population.

The National UFO Reporting Center reports unexplained anonymous sightings of strange lights, flying objects and unusual patterns of objects in central Florida's skies. The Villages in Sumter County, Florida, is no exception. Such sightings are undeniable. Following are just a few of the center's most recent reports by anonymous residents of The Villages:

A bridge view of The Villages at sunset in Sumter County. *Courtesy of CJ Mottin Photography.*

- On April 6, 2014, fifteen red lights were launched into the sky, just like fireworks. After launching, they remained still and then moved up into the clouds. There was no noise.
- Christmas week of 2011, homeowners in The Villages reported UFOs flying directly over their residences. Silver craft shaped like clamshells (they could have been drones), these objects hovered and moved in intelligent patterns of front to back, side to side and zigzags. They only appeared at nightfall and all night long during the two weeks after. They never appeared again.
- On July 22, 2018, a Black Triangle sighting was witnessed as a Villager sat on his porch late one night. As the object entered the stratosphere and Earth's atmosphere, it appeared closer toward the resident, hovered and ascended slowly before taking off.
- On New Year's Eve 2018, a bright white and red light was hidden under the clouds. Then three hovering objects appeared, hovered and left quickly.

An endless stream of retirees continues to migrate to The Villages. According to longevity trends and life expectancy, humans are surviving longer than any other previous generation. Given these trends, The Villages residents are prime examples of elongated life among the masses. Extraterrestrial beings may soon be haunting The Villages for an alternate life form. After all, like gazing into the evening sky, the entertainment is free, every night, in each of The Village's squares, and the company can be very fast.

Along with many clients, friends and family members, I have experienced visions and dreams and welcomed appearances of loved ones after they have passed on. Often this brings much comfort, peace and advice in our time of need.

One of the sweetest spiritual encounters happened recently in The Villages of Sumter County between Mimi Ponzi Fuller and her late husband, Art. This is Mimi's personal account in her own words:

My husband passed last August. A few weeks later, while sleeping on and off in the middle of the night, I saw his light body hovering over me and embracing me. I could feel him kissing my cheek. This lasted only a moment, as the more my mind moved from this state of consciousness and into the awakened state, he disappeared.

A few weeks later, this happened again under the same circumstances, but this time he was trying to speak into my ear. But his speech was inaudible (like a radio station that was losing its frequency and was too scratchy to understand). And again, this was momentary. I asked a friend (who is psychic) if he could tell me what my husband was trying to tell me. My friend told me that my husband was saying "Don't worry. Please KNOW that everything will turn out well for you." Which it did.

A week or so later, under the same circumstances, I got out of bed, left the bedroom, and walked into the kitchen where he was standing. His light body appeared as usual and he outstretched his arms to embrace me again. I moved toward him to embrace him as well. But this time I saw my outstretched arms…and saw my arms in light body. In other words, I was having an out-of-body experience. But the excitement of being reunited with him forced my mind to lose the state of consciousness I was in, and I felt my consciousness get sucked right back into my body. Then I awoke and realized what had happened.

Please note: I teach a once monthly class on the "mind-body-soul connection according to quantum physics," and thus, I have an understanding between levels of consciousness and its relationship to brain activity. There is a level of consciousness that is called "the sweet spot" in between the brain wave levels of low Theta and high Delta. This level is where communication can happen. In the middle of the night, during my "on and off again" sleeping patterns, I experienced this "sweet spot" level.

I haven't seen him in a while now as my sleep pattern is returning to normal. But he continues to alert me during the day from time to time, as exampled by: 1. I hear the doorbell ring. But it's not my current door bell, but rather the doorbell of the first home we lived in together. 2. I hear my cellphone alert me to a text, but the phone is on silent mode and there's never a text. 3. I hear an old-fashioned alarm clock; the kind that winds up, has two bells with the arm that quickly moves back and forth hitting each bell. Haven't seen one of that kind since I was a little girl.

I'd like to describe his light body, as I have never seen this image before. If you could imagine that we have a physical heart with an entire circulatory system and microscopic red blood cells flowing in our arteries, arterioles, and capillaries, he appeared with his Sacred Heart (ball of brilliant light in the center of his torso) with lighted circulatory system, and instead of the red blood cells, the cells were tiny balls or beads of brilliant light circulating all around his being. These circulating beads of light along with his Sacred Heart gave enormous light and glowed to fully see his image. It reveals how "alive" we are in our light body.

After I read Mimi's beautiful love story, I asked her if I could print it in the book and if her late husband's words and actions were familiar to her. This was the reply in her own words:

Yes, he said he would always take care of me, and he still does. There are many examples, but that's a long list. Don't know if you would want me to list it all. Basically, he reminds me (with the examples I've given) if I forgot to lock the front door, or the car in the driveway…or to get a second opinion on financial issues…or to get off my ass and exercise (become strong again)…or accept an invitation to an evening event for my own good even though I don't feel like it…and, most important is…he awakens me at exactly 4:00 a.m. (a few times a week) to remind me to roll over to his side of the bed where my CD player is and to go under the headphones to continue meditation and go into "quantum prayer" for my best possible outcomes....and utilize my light body to heal the destruction that was done to my cells by the sorrow and anxiety that followed this tragedy.

But, bottom line...he continues to help me.

We both agree that with the loss of loved ones, love never dies.

Life lives on in The Villages and can be experienced in many phenomenal ways. Just outside the gated communities, literally right around the corner, past generations, cultures and historical events may lure The Villages residents to step out and uncover the haunted history of Sumter County near the Scenic Sumter Heritage Byway.

PART II

DISCOVERING THE PAST THROUGH PARANORMAL POSSIBILITIES

NEAR THE BYWAY

Please, please bring her back to me…

…Tell her about my big fish story

WILDWOOD HISTORY BRIEFING

For many years, before I moved to central Florida, I visited my parents in The Villages. We loved car rides. Each vacation always included an opportunity to explore The Villages' expansion and the impact on the outside communities. As the new revenues grew, so did the opportunity for historic towns to come alive again. We were witnesses to the future and past of Sumter County.

I was always fascinated with Wildwood. Twenty years ago, I only viewed Wildwood as an old railroad town. During the railroad heyday, sixteen to eighteen freight trains and four passenger trains would shake, rattle and roll within a twenty-four-hour period. It had and still maintains a significant number of historic homes, buildings and businesses in and near the downtown. From the beginning of my visits, Wildwood has transcended from a challenging past into a prime example that the modern-day influences, such as Interstate 75 and The Villages, can bring uplifting opportunities into an established historic community.

The Wildwood area's original residents were the Native Americans. The land itself had no prejudices or preferences. The ideal weather, lush forest and abundant game provided for the generational residents. The land continues to be haunted by the past. Major historic events such as the arrival of European explorers, the War of 1812, the elimination of the Seminoles and the Trail of Tears, Florida statehood and the ending of the Civil War encouraged others to follow into the haunted footsteps of those cultures forced to leave this prime land.

The farmers who came in the 1800s grew cotton and some citrus and other fruits and vegetables. Many found wild oranges living among the pine forests. The citrus may have been planted by Seminoles and other earlier tribes who obtained seeds from the sixteenth-century explorers. History states that the Italian explorer Christopher Columbus brought the first citrus into Florida as early as 1493. By the mid-1500s, the first orange trees had been planted around St. Augustine, Florida. The official land acquisition transfer of Florida from Spain to the United States in 1821 encouraged thousands of prospective planters to move to central Florida to grow citrus.

Legend claims that the name Wildwood was accidentally established by a Western Union surveyor crew in 1877 that may have been lost. It was easy for a crew to get turned around while laying telegraph line in the dense forest. Because of the lush territory, the workmen were required to occasionally report into the main office. Once, after not hearing from them for several days, the main office asked the surveyors to report their whereabouts. One surveyor paused and said, "I don't know, except in the wild woods."

Another possibility is that the name Wildwood is a timeless tribute to the Native Americans who once roamed freely, before outsiders. Once the Europeans and others arrived, the local tribes were almost eradicated. Those remaining were called Seminoles. The name Seminole is derived from the Spanish word *cimarron*, meaning "runaway" or "wild one." Thus, living wild in the woods could have commemorated the Seminoles' legacy to the land.

By 1881, the Wildwood Post Office was operational. The agricultural boom continued, and by 1882, the Tropical Florida Railroad Company had begun service from Ocala into Wildwood. As the railroad lines extended, local produce could be shipped nationally. The most desirable fruits were oranges, lemons and grapefruits. Nearby agricultural settlements, such as Orange Home in 1886, were established to meet the growing demand for citrus.

The city of Wildwood was incorporated in 1889, and the first mayor, Thomas Howell, was elected in 1893. The farming communities in and around the Wildwood area and the downtown flourished, at least until the Great Freeze in the winter of 1894–95.

Mark Andrews's December 25, 1994 article in the *Orlando Sentinel*, "Devastating Great Freeze of 1894–95 Put Squeeze on New Citrus Industry," noted that on the morning of December 29 "cold had settled in to a point where pumps were frozen, water pipes began to burst, foliage blackened and died." Eve Bacon wrote in *Orlando: A Centennial History*, "The temperature dropped to 24 degrees, killing the season's entire citrus crop while most of it still hung on the trees, Christmas Day 1894." Andrews continued, "It was Florida's worst freeze since 1835." Six weeks later, on February 7, the temperature dropped even lower to a deadly seventeen degrees. About 90 percent of the fruit trees were killed. Witnesses said they heard what sounded like pistol shots when the sap froze and blew out the tree bark. Land values plummeted, and many growers were forced to sell at a loss and leave. Some say that the railroad offered free passage for those fleeing this disaster. Some stayed, bought up the bargained priced tracts and expanded into cattle ranching and other farming avenues.

Misfortune continued. In 1889 and again in 1904, fire destroyed much of the main downtown businesses. In 1909, a Sumter County Courthouse fire destroyed any official city records prior to that time. The downtown was rebuilt. But then, in 1912, Wildwood lost its bid for the Sumter County seat to Bushnell by just a handful of votes. Local entrepreneurs' businesses and activities were devastated by the removal of county government revenue.

Despite the setbacks, the railroad and the agricultural industry continued to provide a living for those folks able to stay and work it out. Sadly, in the late 1960s, the struggling railroad industry pulled out of Wildwood. The city could have easily become a virtual ghost town. However, by embracing its past and present possibilities—such as the arrival of Interstate 75, The Villages and many other avenues—Wildwood continues to thrive. An undefinable entrepreneur perseverance permeates beyond time and cultures.

Just like any historic city in flux, there are energies and opportunities to connect with paranormal possibilities.

WILDWOOD DOWNTOWN

When researching an entire county that includes the Sumter Scenic Heritage Byway, it is impossible to investigate every town, park, building, home and more. This is when my intuition comes into play. Most of the locations noted are ones I was psychically led to—and the specific places in downtown Wildwood are no exception.

Haunted sites can be anywhere. When defining hauntings, there are numerous subjective definitions from amateurs and professionals. My years of experience have taught me to break it down and keep it simple. Basically, I operate on two types of hauntings: residual or lasting impressions and active or poltergeist energy. Each can be tuned in or accidentally experienced by one or more of the six senses. Residual energy can be psychically sensed like with the smell of grandma's cookies, a loud cry or a feeling that a spirit has passed through you, just to name a few. Poltergeist energy, contrary to suggestions from media, is rarely evil but usually someone or something in spirit form wanting to be noticed.

Poltergeists can either be tuned into or received by just about anyone. The most common is a spirit tapping, calling or repeating in order to get one's attention. As a trained spiritual medium, I tune in or put on my psychic antennas to see what is revealed to me.

My years of interest in Wildwood come as no surprise to me now. After all, I am writing this book, and the opportunity for some of the city's haunts and history to come alive has now presented itself. There is no selection process, just the belief that I will experience what is meant to be known at this time. By comparing my impressions to history, a historical haunting can then hopefully be justified.

Sometimes the psychic impressions I am receiving are not confirmed, and others are verified right away. As I wander through the downtown of Wildwood now, the intuitive memories returned of my previous perceptions. A strong smell of soot or smoke, injustice, a touch of a boy's hand and a distraught father. The overall psychic impression is very strong for such a small community. The population is nearly 7,000 (as of 2017) and growing. I have experienced parallel feelings only in Charleston, South

Carolina, population about 135,000. The energy is very powerful and may be why I am pulled back to Wildwood over and over again. In each of these cities, Wildwood and Charleston, there exists two strongly opposite residual energies: the willingness to fight for what is right and the cruel acceptance of defeat.

One of the strongest feelings was that of two hangings, one unjustified and one justified, in or near Wildwood. The past isn't so kind to the clashes of contrasting cultures and beliefs.

This first hanging was of George Andrews in 1886. Wildwood would not be incorporated until 1889. The edited version of the story was located at the Genealogy Trails website (http://genealogytrails.com), from the *Hancock Jeffersonian* of Findlay, Ohio, March 15, 1861:

> *A Minister, named George Andrews, a resident of Sumter County, Florida, was lately cited to appear in Court and answer to the charge of improper conduct toward a female relative. Getting into a frenzy on his way to Court, he shot two persons, both of whom died. He was immediately caught by the mob and hung.*

The second source is a more gruesome account derived from the *New York Herald* on March 13, 1861, via newspaperabstracts.com:

> *The occurrence of a bloody tragedy in Sumter County, Florida on the 16th has been briefly noticed. It appears that Rev. George Andrews, pastor of a Methodist church in the county had seduced a young lady, a relative, residing at his house and had also brutally beaten her and for these acts was summoned to appear at Sumter Court House.*
>
> The Augusta Chronicle *further states: For these misdeeds a summons was issued for him to appear at the Court House at Sumterville, before the people, on Saturday, the 16th. Having heard of this, and of the parties who were to serve the summons, Messrs McLendon and Lang, he proceeded to the house of the former and took dinner with the family. After dinner they went to the workshop. Andrews asked McLendon for the loan of his horse to go to Adamsville, which was granted. He had in his possession one double barrel gun, one yauger rifle, two repeaters and two bowie knives.*
>
> *While the horse was being caught a conversation arose about him (Andrews) being summoned before the Regulators. Whereupon Mr. Lang said, "Yes, sir, and here is the summons for you." During this conversation McLendon was mending a pair of shoes. Immediately after Lang's*

answer ANDREWS leveled his gun on MCLENDON, shot him in the side, and killed him instantly. Turning around quickly, he leveled his gun to shoot LANG with the other barrel. LANG knocked up the gun and received the whole load in the palm of his right hand. LANG then picked up ANDREWS' yauger, to shoot him (ANDREWS), but could not cock it on account of his shattered hand, threw down the gun and ran. As he ran ANDREWS shot him through the left wrist with a repeater.

A Mr. HYATT, in the shop at the time, picked up the yauger, ran off about thirty yards and leveled it at ANDREWS, but the latter was too quick, and shot HYATT with his repeater, grazing him on the shoulder. HYATT shot, but missed. Hereupon ANDREWS took after LANG and pursued him about two hundred yards. Not being able to overtake him, he returned to the shop, reloaded his guns, and proceeded over to Mr. CONDRAY's, about one mile distant.

At CONDRAY's gate ANDREWS met Dr. MCHENRY, whom he told he was tired and very thirsty, and wanted a drink of water, stepping inside the yard, and seeing Mr. CONDRAY talking to a negro boy, he observed, "I have commenced my work, and right here I intend to finish it."

Whereupon he leveled his gun and shot CONDRAY through the bowels, who only lived about four hours.

Rev. Mr. PARKER being present, seized the murderer from behind and held him fast until MCHENRY came to his assistance. As the doctor caught hold of ANDREWS, the latter presented his gun to the doctor's breast, who warded it off, and the load went into the ground. He was then tied and confined until next morning under strict guard.

The news having been circulated in the neighborhood, a large number of citizens assembled at CONDRAY's house. After due deliberation, he was sentenced to be hanged, and about twelve o'clock ____ he was hanged accordingly, sixty or seventy citizens of the county signing his death warrant. There was not a dissenting voice on the ground. The last words of this hardened wretch were, "I am only sorry that I did not kill three or four more."

The second hanging was more than one hundred years later after Reverend Andrews's demise. Sadly, Jesse Woods's story could still happen today. By relaying the exact words of his 1956 tragedy, as reported and located at the Genealogy Trails website (from the *Spokesman-Review* of October 29, 1956), humanity can pause and realize that Jesse died a senseless death. Hopefully he did not die in vain:

Negro Feared Victim of Florida Lynching
Wildwood, Fla., Oct. 28.—A Negro man, 28, was taken from his blood-spattered police station cell by unknown persons today under circumstances indicating he may have been the victim of a lynch mob.

More than 150 state and local officers, aided by airplanes and bloodhounds, searched through woods and fields surrounding this central Florida town without finding any immediate trace of the missing man.

He is Jesse Woods, who recently returned here after spending several years in the north. He was arrested last night on a drunk and disorderly charge after he reportedly created a disturbance in a grocery and addressed a remark, "Hey, there, Honey," to a white woman.

Woods was arrested shortly before 6 p.m. yesterday by Police Chief Ed Mullis and locked up in the town's tiny jail, a one-story frame structure located across the street from a movie theater in the center of the town's business section. About four hours after the arrest, Woods was freed on a $50 cash bond put up by his Father, who operated a small truck farm about five miles from town. The father and Woods left the jail and walked to the father's car, parked nearby, but returned to the jail in a few minutes, asserting some white persons were following them and they were "scared." Mullis said that the father asked him to resume custody of Woods for Woods' protection. Mullis said he agreed and locked up Woods for a second time. Mullis said that Woods disappeared from the jail between midnight and 1 a.m. when the jail door was found open, its lock forced. Mullis told reporters that a lot of people had been coming out of the movie theater at the time the elder Woods went to the jail to free his son. He said some of these may have shouted or jeered at the new Negros. Reports had been circulating throughout the evening that the jail contained a Negro prisoner who had "insulted" a white woman.

History and haunts can be quite profound and heartbreaking. Cruelty to one another will never be justified. It is, however, necessary to realize that the past can repeat itself. Spirits speak out, sometimes to tell us what we don't necessarily want to hear but other times to encourage us in some positive ways.

What is a spirit anyway? I recently talked to jeweler Rayne Rankin, owner of JailHouse Jeweler in downtown Wildwood. His previous business location was housed inside the 1926 city jail. As far as he knows, his previous business location was the first official jail. He loves the jailhouse building and its unique stone structure. Moving his business was difficult. Being an old soul, and given the history, he feels a real connection to the old jail.

Rayne specializes in jewelry and watch repair. He also sells estate items, including clocks. I asked him if he ever thought that a clock could be haunted. He chuckled a bit and said, "Well, now that you mention it…." He went on to tell me about a recent acquisition of an old clock. Familiar to chimes, ticks and such, he said, "This clock in particular seemed to be chiming when there was no inside parts." He continued, "If this clock did chime, it wouldn't sound like the chime I heard."

We talked about the large range of businesses located in the downtown. A trip through Wildwood's unique downtown affords one the opportunity to eat, shop and find just about anything. After reviewing the offerings and the history, we both came to a similar conclusion. Certain locations in downtown could be haunted for disaster and others energized for success. It's well worth the trip on your way down the Scenic Sumter Heritage Highway to find out for yourself. Given the shaky history of the past and the tenacious spirit of the people, like Rayne's business, time will tell!

Roosters on Oxford

Have you ever noticed that there are times when you are led to a place that you never knew existed, and when you arrive, it feels like home? Roosters on Oxford is home to me now.

Owner Tami Roosa recently opened the coffeehouse, serving organic coffee along with gluten-free fresh-baked goodies. She also sells vintage furniture and knickknacks. Inside and outside of the 1902 Craftsman historic site is a delight to all your senses, including the sixth sense—a spirited, homey atmosphere with yummy delights. Roosa admitted that she was somehow mystically led to find her "one-of-a-kind place." Quite by accident, of course.

I was introduced to Roosters on Oxford by Jacqueline Naja and her husband, Steve. They are residents of the Village of Desoto in The Villages. Jacqueline had invited me to be a guest at an upcoming ladies' social event for her ladies of Desoto. I was asked to entertain the ladies with quick palm, cards or energy readings. The get-togethers would be two Friday mornings in a row at Roosters on Oxford in Wildwood. Before the events, I had never heard of the location but knew (through Jacqueline) that it was an upscale coffee shop in downtown Wildwood.

Jacqueline and I had arranged to meet at the coffee shop a few days before the scheduled events. We wanted to plan the agenda on site, and knowing my background, she was curious what I would psychically experience when I arrived at the historic Roosters on Oxford.

I arrived early to allow myself time to walk around before Jacqueline's arrival. Right away, as I stepped from the car, several strong entities were pushing me, literally out of the car, across the street and right up the sidewalk to the front porch. I felt like Dorothy being pushed into seeing the Wizard of Oz.

Roosters on Oxford is an unexpected delight! I had no idea it was a 1902 Craftsman historic home. The exterior porch is huge and so inviting. It is smartly decorated with eclectic, repurposed furniture and

Roosters on Oxford: Vintage Coffee House & Furnishings. *Author's collection.*

artwork, all cleverly arranged for a nice porch sit. Photographs do not do justice to the 1902 home. It has an indescribable homey charm inside and out!

As I entered for the first time, I paused on the steps. The historic residence took my breath away, and I felt an immediate kinship with the spirits and location. I turned around and faced the front yard. Unexpectedly, my reoccurring vision of a Wildwood lynching came back to me. I carefully stepped back down the stairs and slowly walked over to the huge oak tree on the corner of the massive lot. Could one of the hangings have happened here? Or nearby? I was out of breath.

I needed some balance. I grabbed and hugged the tree, tightly, for grounding. As I did, an entirely different scene came to life. It was cheerful—not a hanging, thank goodness.

Children were running around playing and laughing. Their clothing indicated that it would have been around the early 1900s. I smiled at the happy scene, and then I was drawn to look back at the house. In the upstairs window, I saw a middle-aged man, probably in his forties or fifties, with dark hair. He seemed to be leaning heavily against the window as he watched the children play. The kids were oblivious to his overwhelming sadness. He seemed distraught and distracted. As I locked eyes with his energy, he pleaded, "Please, please bring her home [back] to me."

As is my custom, I immediately acknowledged the troubled soul. I assured him that I would do what I could to bring him some answers and comfort. I knew that it was a female he was yearning for. What happened to her? Was she ill? Had she died or simply vanished? Was it his wife or daughter? Time, hopefully, would bring the answers we needed to console this spirit.

By this time, Jacqueline had arrived. I relayed the information to her. You never know for whom the messages are intended—or who will be able to assist. After our business meeting, I met with the owner, Tami Roosa. She shared some of the history of the home and her own story, as well as how she had accidentally found the house (or rather how the house found her). The haunting images I had experienced were shared with her. She, like me, is determined to find the answers.

The Baker House

From the very first time I stepped inside the historic Baker House, I just knew that there was something very special about the historic homestead. In all my paranormal investigations, I have never felt such an overwhelming feeling of love and sweetness materialize from a home and its people.

Psychically engaged, I eagerly walked up to the front of the Baker House. I took a deep breath, released it and was immediately immersed in my first paranormal investigation of the home. I noticed that the front wooden door was open, but the old screen door was closed. I was beckoned to come closer. Immediately, I felt such a warm welcome that I swear I was lifted up off the ground and delivered right on the front porch.

The enthusiastic husband-and-wife spirits were delightfully poised right inside the screen door. Like an old-fashioned postcard, the couple stood, smiling and laughing. They were so happy to be together again. Their arms were lovingly wrapped around each other's waists. Dressed and groomed for visitors, her luminescent gown sparkled in the dancing sunlight, and he was quite dapper in his tailored afternoon waistcoat.

The Baker House is a living legacy of love! *Courtesy of SSHB–Tangent Media.*

Graciously, they ushered me inside to the foyer of the Baker House. I stopped and looked around at the comfortable but elegant surroundings. It felt like being inside a dollhouse. Everything seemed to glisten, and I could detect the smell of freshly applied furniture polish. A slight flowery fragrance lingered in the air. As we stood there, I heard a small boy's voice call down from upstairs: "Don't forget to tell her about my big fish story." He was quite insistent and announced it several times until we all acknowledged him. Then the couple merely vanished into thin air.

My investigation continued on the first floor. The rooms were smartly arranged with fine furniture pieces and exquisite whatnots. In the front parlor, an antique chair and table set seemed to be the perfect place for a spot of fine tea. A large ornate mirror in the corner beckoned, casting interesting energy vibes. Mesmerized, I walked like a zombie toward the reflective piece. I peered deeply into the looking glass. Several faces were looking back at me. Some were very young, and some were very old.

Since my first visit, several docents and I have identified a young boy and an elegant older woman dressed in black. Further self-reflection may bring many new experiences and lives into focus.

I walked back into the foyer and started up the elegant stairwell. I wanted to locate the young boy who had so eloquently spoken to us. As I ascended, the late afternoon sun danced and filtered through the landing's colorful stained-glass window. A rainbow of colors danced on the walls. I felt I was in a dream. "Be careful" I was told. I then experienced a strong descending sound of *thump thump thump* on the stairs as I turned the final corner to the upstairs bedrooms.

If was as if the Bakers had never left. The warm feeling of family and business encased me. I was in love with the Baker House, and I had only been here a few minutes.

The first room on the left was the adorable nursery room. It was sweetly decorated and smelled of babies and fresh flowers. Then my energy was immediately drawn to the young child's picture on the wall. Impishly, he was looking down at me, and I knew it was the charming boy I had heard. His smile was contagious. I gave him a smile and walked around to the other three bedrooms.

The front feminine bedroom was quite beautiful. A maternal, warm and cozy feeling floated among the fancy furnishings and decorations. The two back bedrooms were quite a mixture of energy and décor. The first sported a massive masculine bedroom set. The second back bedroom had a mixture of costuming and period clothing among the eclectic fine pieces. A wide variety of residual energies played on my senses.

In the clothing room, I was drawn to the large closet overflowing with dresses, mostly wedding gowns. I felt an attachment of a gown to the previous wearer. It didn't belong to her or the Bakers. Indeed, I felt that the bride-to-be had been left at the altar.

I admired the many bedroom furnishings but felt no immediate psychic impressions at the time. I decided to continue my tour downstairs. After I arrived back downstairs, I headed out the back door of the main homestead. Immediately, I felt a rush of energy and witnessed horses with riders speeding by me. *Whish!* My hair was blown into my face, and then they were gone! The group was oblivious to me as they trotted down the road.

On the side lawn there stood the most magnificent oak tree, more than two hundred years old I was told later. I also felt the presence of an African American man. Quite loud and boisterous, perhaps singing or repeating lines in a deep baritone voice. He was among a large group of people.

I wandered back to the second building of the home. This addition housed the dining room, kitchen and quarters for the help. By this time, the house's divine energy had me spinning. I needed to sit down. This is my best account of my first official paranormal investigation of the Baker House. The residual graciousness of the Bakers lives on. It is easy to get attached to this spirited house and the family.

I sat down and gathered my notes and thoughts. I was ready to share my initial medium impressions with the docents. Before my visit inside, I knew very little of their history or the family except that the house dated back to the late 1800s and that many generations of the Bakers resided here until 2012. What could history confirm of my own psychic impressions?

Senator David Hume Baker, along with his wife, Mary Hannah Mathis Baker, and their teenage son, David Mathis, arrived in Sumter County, Florida, in 1886. The senator chose the Orange Home, Florida area (present-day Wildwood) to settle in and raise citrus. He was a state senator in Kentucky and later in Florida. Coming from Muhlenberg County, Kentucky, the Bakers brought many southern traditions with them. With love and determination, this first generation of Florida Bakers began to create a solid foundation to be business and political powerhouses in the Florida community. Many of their traditions continue today.

The senator and his family started building the grand residence around 1886. It took several years to complete, so the family lived in a small Cracker-style home that once stood just west of the big house. Completed in 1890, the new home consists of a two-story main house with porches on both floors and a separate two-story kitchen house. The house was once topped with a cupola that could be reached by a ladder that once stood in the large open attic. Each building was connected by a covered walkway. Much of the main house is original, including the beautiful wooden floors, gas lighting, sash windows, the ornate and detailed door hinges, the hand-carved stair railing and most of the stained-glass window on the second-floor landing.

A few of the antiques inside are original to the home and family. Family photographs, clothing, china, linen and such are tastefully displayed among the family and donated furnishings. In 2012, the Baker homestead and five acres were given to the City of Wildwood. Since then, Parks and Recreation manager Dennis Andrews and an outstanding group of volunteers, including the docents, continue to lovingly restore this magnificent home.

The City of Wildwood Parks and Recreation website describes the homestead so beautifully: "The Baker House has stood for over 100 years and has seen the world around it change. It has been home to six generations of Bakers and a mainstay in the community. It is a true testament to the craftsmanship of days gone by, to the love and care of many family members and a piece of the City of Wildwood History."

Historic, Christmas and haunted tours; murder mysteries; Victorian teas; weddings; and special events such as the Heritage Festival are some of the many ways that the Baker House volunteers continue to donate their time and talent to raise the needed funds to keep this grand lady a living legend of the area.

Two of the outstanding volunteers are devoted docents Tanya Mikeals and Beth Crouch-Payne. These ladies work endlessly and lovingly as docents, actresses, organizers and more—any part, anywhere, if something needed to help to restore, maintain and show off the beautiful Baker House. These remarkable women are local to the area and are familiar and friendly with the history and living Baker family.

On my first official paranormal investigation, they were present along with Cheryl Trask and possibly others. They were able to confirm the history for many of the psychic medium impressions I received. Keep in mind that I knew almost nothing of the Baker House and the family history.

The Bakers have always been known for their true sense of hospitality and graciousness in all they do. Family, business and community continue to be vital parts of the Baker legacy. All were welcome into their home. In fact, most homes built at the time would have featured a fine dining room in the main house. While designing his new residence, Senator Baker created his

Elegant Christmas tours by docents Tanya Mikeals and Beth Crouch-Payne. *Courtesy of Crouch-Payne and Mikeals' collection.*

own "man cave," and thus the elegant dining room was placed in the second building, so "his" and "her" friends could be accommodated.

David Mathis, along with his lovely wife, Lorena Dimmick, were the second generation of the Bakers in Florida. They had three sons: Paul died as an infant, and Laurence, born in 1900, was quite a joy, especially to his oldest brother, David Lewis Baker, born in 1897. The family enjoyed their aquatic vacations away from the hard work of the homestead.

Just like typical children, the brothers enjoyed water activities during their vacation. Sometimes while diving directly into water from the jon boat, mischievous boys don't necessarily look before they leap. They are unaware of what dangers could lie below the water's surface. One summer day in 1910, Laurence was playing. We can imagine him laughing as he dove straight into the water without looking and unexpectedly landed on a "big fish."

He was immediately attacked and barbed by a stingray. Despite the family's best efforts, he died immediately. The family was heartbroken and full of despair. He was gently brought back home and, a few days later, buried at the Adamsville Cemetery. Given his unexpected and early demise, Laurence perhaps lives on at the Baker House. He is eternally grateful to play at his loving home and apparently is eager to share his big fish story.

The story of the young lady not related to the Bakers who did not marry is true. She was present at the first investigation but wishes to remain anonymous. The residual psychic impression took her by surprise. Smiling, she confirmed it all! She has indeed worn that wedding dress from the Baker House closet for fundraising events. The gown is not hers or theirs. It was donated. She is so grateful that fate took care of her that day so many years ago so she could be so happy today.

Remember the warning to "be careful" and the *thump thump thump* on the stairs? A family member or two and others have often experienced Gladys or "Mumu." She was the third-generation Mrs. Baker. The residual energy and antics of Mumu and her cane are often experienced, as she still carefully navigates the stairs since her death in 1993.

The Bakers' downstairs parlor mirror still fascinates me. More and more interesting impressions and reflections are being revealed. The antique looking glass often sports some interesting spirits looking out, while others are gazing in. Self-reflection can certainly draw an audience.

The outside horseback riders represented generations of the Bakers. Horsemanship was important and enjoyable to all generations of the Bakers.

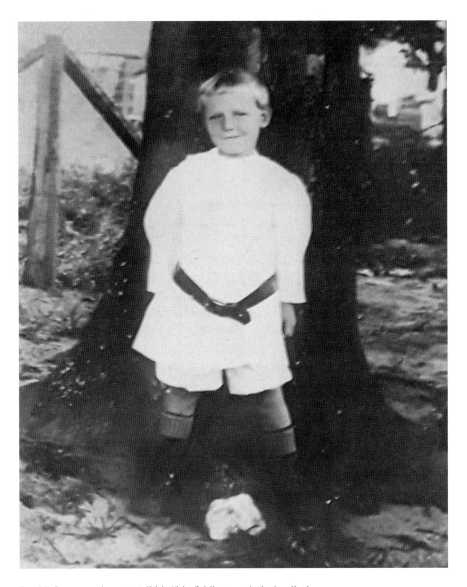

Impish Laurence loves to tell his "big fish" story. *Author's collection.*

After the late 1800s freeze, the Bakers turned to cattle farming and have often been seen spiritually riding their mounts down the road. The most recent generations that lived in the home, according to one of the local docents, rode their horses into Leesburg to eat at a local hamburger joint. Drive-up

Thump, thump, thump. Mumu's here! "Be careful!" she says. *Author's collection.*

service on horseback—what an interesting concept! Haunted history does indeed ride on at the Baker House.

The story about the large African American man had the docents in a conundrum, as the Bakers never had any slaves. In fact, Senator Baker served on the Union side in the Civil War. The large man with a loud voice appearing on the property was indeed a puzzle. But then a most unusual memory was recalled.

Back in the 1982, Roger Inman Productions spent several days filming a Big Ben Rice commercial for the Masins of Paris Corporation on the Baker House property. The larger-than-life African American male character was the featured actor. His name wasn't given in the newspaper, but the featured photographs depict the actor. He is sitting and standing high among many others while the commercial was filmed. Gladys and David Lewis Baker, third-generation residents at the time, had opened their home to the film crew. Featured extras included local children and students, along with some farm hands, from Orlando. The production created quite a stir at the homestead. As it was filmed near a public road, hundreds rubbernecked as they drove by, and even more stopped to see what was going on. The commercial production only appeared in European markets. The official paparazzi weren't present that day, but paranormally, it makes quite a charming follow-up.

Others have experienced paranormal activities at the Baker House— family teacup energy, stairway and upper-floor spirits that may sit on the bed with you or brush by a shoulder or cheek and an eager ghost pup. Such poltergeist activity is sometimes confused with negative Hollywood displays. This can sometimes drive participants away and not toward this family's astonishing history and home. I prefer to lovingly experience all avenues of the many generations that reside at the Baker House and keep their history alive.

"The Baker family had the foresight to preserve the impact they had on this area and their history for future generations." *Author's collection.*

The most endearing generational tradition brought by the Bakers from Kentucky is that of a simple flower. The first Floridian, Mrs. Baker, insisted that a camellia bush cutting from her Kentucky home be brought down and planted on her new homestead. Baker tradition lovingly mandates that each Baker bride wears or carries the family's heirloom flower at her own wedding. The original camellia bush, along with a second generation (2012), has been well pampered so that this sweet Baker bridal tradition can continue at the Baker House in Sumter County, Florida.

Esther Bulger, another charming and dedicated Baker House volunteer, recently directed the Baker House's first Victorian teas. At the closing of the tea, she thanked all for attending, volunteer and participants alike, and kindly shared, "They say you live forever if you are remembered. The Baker family had the foresight to preserve the impact they had on this area and their history for future generations."

The Baker House will live on spiritually and historically to be a perfect visit in Sumter County, Florida, near the Scenic Sumter Heritage Byway.

COLEMAN, CENTER HILL AND OTHER GHOST TOWN ODDITIES

After experiencing city and homestead life, it is always refreshing to return to the rural beauty of the backroads of Sumter County. Around each bend, a supernatural or natural event may be found before or during the drive down the Scenic Sumter Heritage Byway. There are living ghost towns, such as Coleman and Center City, that created quite a stir during their heyday. Loosely using the term "ghost towns" for some of the smaller hamlets doesn't necessarily mean that they are deserted. They are simply less traveled. Truth be told, most of their residents enjoy it that way.

The Coleman area was settled around 1882 and named after B.R. Coleman. It was the springs in the Coleman area that brought settlers after the Civil War. Warm Springs Hammock lands near Coleman and can produce twenty-five thousand gallons of water per minute.

Oranges, cotton, cattle, sheep and hogs were grown or raised. When the stagecoach line was replaced by the railroad, the area developed into the chartered community of Coleman in 1925. At one time, the town was so prosperous that it owned its own telephone system and was boasted as the "Cabbage Capital of the World."

Downtown Coleman is very small and quiet now. However, it is worth the stop to view a ghost town within the town's limits. What was once a tourist stop, a historic village attraction, can be viewed through a locked fence enclosure. Inside is housed an 1849 post office, an 1895 train depot, an 1869 schoolhouse and a 1913 jail. Some claim that the ghost village attraction contains more actual historic buildings in one location than can be found anywhere else in Sumter County, Florida.

I peered through the fence and walked around the perimeter. I felt the isolation and emptiness of a time long gone. It reminded me of what I found chiseled on several graves in Sumter County: "Gone but not forgotten."

Perhaps someday someone will be able to bring Coleman's ghost village attraction back to life. There certainly are some enterprising opportunities among the raw beauty of the enchanting countryside.

Some days I travel alone, at least without living spirits. One day, my psychic antennas were tuned in so strongly that I almost missed the county's original seat of Sumterville, named after General Thomas Sumter, an American Revolutionary War hero. The early cemetery sits timelessly among the busy roads, holding deep its secrets and family lore. I take a moment to walk among the many who sacrificed their lives for the land. Another phantom ghost town of what was, respected and left in restful tranquility.

Sumterville's heritage is commemorated by its representation on the Scenic Sumter Heritage Byway. A few friendly cemetery spirits acknowledge my visit. It will be interesting to see how their stories may play out in the future. Being eternally peaceful doesn't mean that it is past its prime. The ghosts may be patiently waiting for just the right opportunity for the spirit to speak so their history can be retold.

I travel farther south and psychically witness a family's 1960s light-colored station wagon careening down the road. The automobile is out of control, and the family inside is screaming for the driver to slow down. Just as quickly as I witness this heart-stopping paranormal impression, the car vanishes. I pull over to settle my nerves. Despite this event, the area is breathtakingly beautiful. Groves of oak trees and pines provide a serene feeling as my heart slows down.

I return to the truck, hop inside and continue farther south. Suddenly, I hear a screeching cry. The superhuman screams pierce the dead country air. I am driving fast so I slow down, turn around, cross back over the small bridge and notice the sign: Jumper Creek. The shrieks and yipping echo up and down the creek bed. Could this be the sounds of a phantom wild swamp beast or perhaps a spirited Seminole warrior?

The pulsating energy runs chills up and down my arms and legs. The lingering feeling is quite disarming. Perhaps it is time to turn off the psychic antennas and concentrate on my driving. When the timing is right, I hope to discover or uncover some type of historical facts to confirm my haunted encounters.

What I realized later is quite interesting. The Jumper family name is an integral part of the Seminole people's past and living legacy of Florida, including Sumter County. A more prophetic and mystical meaning of the Native American's cry will soon be revealed on our travels down the Scenic Sumter Heritage Byway.

The creek also leads into the many waterways that the Green Swamp monster has been known to haunt. Either way, the wild cries certainly seemed real to me.

The 1960s station wagon and its passengers are still baffling. I have searched newspapers far and wide, but so far there's no news of our frantic family. Hopefully the car was able to slow down and stop among the many shaded picnic areas on the Byway for a nice family outing.

With Sumter County leading the nation in the early 1900's in string beans, cabbage, and cucumbers, vegetable packing sheds were numerous.

The "String Bean Capital of the World." *Courtesy of SSHB–Tangent Media.*

Palatlakaha/Old Abrahams Town (or Pilaklikaha/Abraham's Town). Recent archaeological finds have uncovered this town's buried past. *Courtesy of SSHB–Tangent Media.*

Center Hill is nearby and houses a haunted past among the rich land. Once named the "String Bean Capital of the World," this farming community continues to maintain a wholesomeness of privacy among its living history past. The original settlement was renamed by either the postmaster, Thomas W. Spicer, or Mrs. Carrie Lovell around the 1830s or so. Mrs. Lovell stated that the designation seemed appropriate, considering how it was stationed "in the center of the county and on top of a hill."

The area's past runs deeper than the 1800s. Perhaps the Native American cry I heard was an introduction to the area's original residents, whose unfortunate past is buried deep within this fertile farmland.

There were many names before Center Hill: most notably Abraham's Town or Pilaklikaha. The area was originally called Old Abrahams Town after Abraham, a former slave who later served as a recruiter and interpreter for the Seminoles.

By the 1800s, Black Seminoles and fugitive slaves had peacefully settled in Old Abrahams Town and renamed it Pilaklikaha. For only a few short decades, the residents maintained a fulfilling native village life. Around 1826, the United States and Florida governments heard about the lush environment and wanted to claim the area's "finest land" for themselves and future development. Caught in the crossfire, the distraught natives fled. Most moved into the Wahoo Swamp. Their village was destroyed by the government; Pilaklikaha was no more.

Almost two hundred years later, the land continues to provide. Nowadays, neighborly citizens in Center Hill prefer their private lifestyle to high-density developments and big-city challenges. A lush agriculture still thrives among the many who now live peacefully among the haunted past on the Scenic Sumter Heritage Byway.

PART III
SEMINOLE MAGIC, MYSTICISM AND MASSACRE

ON THE BYWAY

I see the happy Seminole children running by…

In my mind's eye, he stands, tall and proud. He extends his arms out, across the land and up toward the sky. A supernatural energy expels from his extended fingers and the deed is done. Forevermore…

SEMINOLE HISTORY BRIEFING

As one enters the official Scenic Sumter Heritage Byway, among the splendor of the natural beauty lies a supernatural warning that not all seems as it appears. The Byway, like other backroads in Sumter County, is covered by noble trees, hallowed grounds and an undeniable energy of a tainted, haunted history.

As the ice age receded thousands of years ago, the First Nations people roamed across the continent, and certain tribes established themselves among the fertile grounds of central Florida. Sumter County's original natives dwelled in these lands for thousands of years until others found a way to interrupt, corrupt and destroy their way of life.

The invasion of Spain and others left just a few natives. Those remaining were coined "Seminoles." The Seminole people comprised the remaining indigenous Native American tribes, many of Creek origin and additional cultures, such as African American freed and runaway slaves.

The traditional Seminole way of life was a balance of duties. Women guided the daily village life, including child rearing, cooking, cleaning and farming, while men were carefully selected and trained for their specific fighting or hunting skills. Whether nomadic or not, each clan had a designated chief and sometimes an additional medicine man. Spiritually, the Seminoles operated through nature, rituals, highly trained skills and strong leadership.

THE FIRST SEMINOLE WAR

Up until about two hundred years ago, the Florida territory was pure wilderness. Clean rivers and lush forests provided a home to deer, bears, a few white settlers and a few thousand Seminoles. Escaped and freed slaves also found refuge and often were taken in by the Seminoles. Some intermarried and formed their own societies. In 1817–18, Florida was still owned by Spain, but the onslaught of white settlers, slave hunters and others continued to intrude on the land of the Seminoles.

The United States and Florida governments wanted Florida cleared of all the white settlers' enemies. The First Seminole War had begun! The natives resisted. More whites migrated from other states when Spain sold Florida to the United States. The Seminoles continued to defend themselves. The new immigrants demanded that the government step in and eradicate the Seminoles and their allies. Andrew Jackson came with his soldiers, built forts, cleared roads and tried to force the Seminoles out. Many runaway slaves were recaptured and returned to their owners or killed.

The natives continued to fight for their land. The government, led by Andrew Jackson, signed the Indian Removal Act. Later, in 1834, after years of conflict, the Payne's Landing Treaty ratification was underhandedly authorized. The treaty itself was somewhat questionable. Even some of the United States soldiers testified that tricky wording and empty promises

The Seminoles'
magic lives on.
*Courtesy of SSHB–
Tangent Media.*

had the chiefs "wheedled and bullied into signing" such an agreement. The Seminoles had somehow authorized the United States government to permanently remove them from their land claims and resettle them into an established Indian territory west of the Mississippi.

Tricked, deceived and disheartened, the Seminole Nation had no choice. The Second Seminole War began in 1835 at what is now the site of Dade Battlefield State Park in Sumter County on the Scenic Sumter Heritage Byway.

DADE BATTLEFIELD HISTORIC STATE PARK

When we arrived in the central Florida area, I had no idea of the impact of the Seminole people right outside my backdoor. In fact, Larry and I stumbled across the Dade County state park quite by accident.

We had purchased a foreclosure and, for the first year, concentrated on rebuilding the homestead. Larry loves to invent, build and rebuild. His talents are evident in and outside our home. His outside barbecue center included plans for a pizza baker. Locally, he had found and ordered a specific bottom metal plate for the oven. When it was ready, we forged down some backroads to pick it up. As we were carefully gauging our direction in the rural area, a sign appeared: "The Dade Battlefield Historic State Park." What was that all about? Once again, fate had stepped in.

Dade Battlefield Historic State Park was our initial introduction to the history found along the scenic Byway in Sumter County. Given Larry's Cherokee heritage and our paranormal interests, this trip unknowingly sparked the idea of *Haunted Sumter County, Florida*, including future visits to the state park.

Mankind's "survival of the fittest" is often sadly marred by the malicious massacre of many people and cultures. The brutal forced departure demanded by Payne's Landing Treaty once again threatened the Seminoles' existence in Florida. The fate of the Seminoles was continually and fiercely fought over. This battle was no exception. Major Dade and his men had little chance of survival.

It was a cold winter's day on December 23, 1835, when Major Francis Langhorne Dade and his 108 soldiers left Fort Brooke. The one-hundred-mile march from Tampa Bay took them to Fort King near present-day Ocala. It was slow progress across primitive roads. The regiment was adequately armed with guns and a cannon. Great precautions had been taken against native attacks, including the use of an advance guard and flankers to warn and possibly ward off nightly Seminole raids.

The soldiers were three quarters of the way down the road, unaware that the Seminoles had been tracking their progress. The Seminole warriors had patiently calculated each step of their battle plan.

Early in the cold morning of the sixth day, the soldiers had buttoned up their coats tightly over their ammunition boxes. Major Dade had sent the advance guard ahead but had kept the flankers at camp. Trained to expect night assaults, Major Dade never expected a daylight attack, especially in the open pine woods.

As the whooping and hollering commenced from the war party, the soldiers were unprepared to meet the onslaught of the Seminoles. The battle raged for hours. Time and time again the Seminoles attacked. By the day's end, all but three of the soldiers had been killed. The Second Seminole War had begun.

The repercussions of such a massacre angered the white settlers and the United States government further. The fury prevailed for seven more years. The conflict was bitter, and the Seminoles' fate was sealed. There was no peace treaty or armistice in play. In 1842, roughly three thousand Seminoles were forcibly removed from Florida and traveled the Trail of Tears to the Indian Territory, which is now Oklahoma. A few Seminoles remained in Florida and scattered, mostly south. The land was now fully available to the white settlement.

As sensitive as mediums and psychics can be, injustices can be quite overwhelming. My first attendance of the Dade Battle, replayed on such sacred land, was no exception. As Larry and I sat there, I felt the beat of my husband's own Cherokee heart. As the actors spoke and the warfare got underway, my own heart skipped a few beats. My fears played out psychic visuals of many battles and injustices. Time and time again. Every emotion felt by each side was replaying in my mind. I blinked several times, tears rolling down my check, and I said silent prayers.

And then the sunlight beamed down as the lingering smoke from the cannons and gunfire rose up. I witnessed the residual energy of raising souls. For a moment, stillness prevailed. All was calm. The battle was over that day, but the impact remains on this haunted land and in my mind.

Souls arising from the Dade Battlefield State Park reenactment. *Author's collection.*

A 2019 January program printed by the Dade Battlefield Society featured an article, "The Reason Why." The essay concludes by encouraging each of us to be responsible citizens: "The fields that were battlegrounds have become the nation's playground. Money, lives, and honor paid for this land. Perhaps now it is our responsibility to plant instead of cut. To protect instead of kill. To see that the rivers again run clean. We cannot undo the past, but we can study it, learn from it and in so doing honor the sacrifices of all races."

As we left that day, I once again clocked into an unexplainable supernatural force. On my first visit and on several visits after, I had recognized and acknowledged this strange mystic manifestation. Who was this sage and why was his residual energy still so powerful? His identity, like other mysteries, would have to wait. First I needed to make a few detours on the Byway.

WAHOO SWAMP

I met Martin Steele at my first Scenic Sumter Heritage Byway meeting. I was seeking advice and permission. The group was incredibly helpful. One of the Byway members, Martin, a local resident and writer, was curious about my psychic working technique. He volunteered to meet me and Larry in Bushnell to show us the area and witness my skills. Except for a quick drive-by of downtown Bushnell a few weeks before, I was unfamiliar with the history and happenings of the area.

Witnessing someone's hometown through a psychic's eyes can be quite interesting. The idea of driving a psychic around and waiting for impressions to engage can be challenging—my endless chatter, questions, quick turns, sudden stops and watching my physical or mental reaction. Yes, it can be quite annoying.

At this point in my writings, the perceptions and research were starting to come together in some other regions of the county. My travels with Martin that day included more than a few turns down unknown roads. I was open to receive, and during the ride, many perceptions were indeed being received—elephants, bank robbers and more.

I saw the happy Seminole children running by…

In addition to the children's playful antics, I noticed a grandmotherly figure leaning against a tree. She was keeping a watchful eye on the young natives at play—a very peaceful and loving memory.

Martin turned a corner. Right away, the energy dramatically changed. I knew I was at Wahoo Swamp. Martin had been careful to not turn down a road that displayed the Wahoo sign. He confirmed that we were indeed at Wahoo Swamp.

I was completely tuned into my surroundings. I smelled blood. I saw several dead Seminoles on the ground. A brutal fight had taken place. I could sense the natives high in the trees and low among the large roots of the trees. Soldiers were here. No mercy.

I got out of the car immediately. I stood for a while right in the middle of the road, absorbing all the energy around me. There was much being said and planned by the spirits around me. It was an overwhelming feeling. I needed to disengage myself from this force. I knew that I would be returning. So, for now, I quieted my mind and returned to the car. The initial observations would be carefully studied and compared with historical accounts.

According to history, the Black Seminoles, often including runaway slaves, occupied many small villages along the Withlacoochee River just outside Wahoo Swamp. Despite the many outside challenges, it was a happy village life for many. The large swamp area was the stronghold of the Indians. Mostly farmers, provisions, cattle and their families were sometimes hidden among the safety of the Wahoo Swamp. Slave traders, soldiers and others wanted to recapture the slaves, steal their cattle and goods and remove the remaining natives.

Almost a year after the Dade Battle, the Second Seminole War continued in the Wahoo Swamp. A plan had been launched by the U.S. Army and others to raid the Seminoles' supplies and destroy the villages. The local villagers, forewarned, had fled to safer grounds in anticipation of the attacks.

Here in the Wahoo Swamp area, there were several brutal encounters between the army and Creek mercenaries against the Seminoles, led by Chiefs Osuchee and Yaholooche. Despite the large numbers of soldiers and their counterparts, some estimates being over 550, it took only a few hundred of the Seminole warriors to keep the soldiers at bay. Some Seminoles trapped in the swamp were somehow able to escape and ghost the enemy.

Despite the overwhelming odds, only ten warriors among the many soldiers lay dead in Wahoo Swamp. Was it magic that day that protected the Seminoles?

Years later, the Third Seminole War raged farther south between 1855 until 1858. It consisted of several skirmishes led by Seminole leader Billy Bowlegs. By the end of 1858, Billy Bowlegs had finally agreed to leave Florida. This left a small band of Seminoles under the command of Abiaka (also known as Aripiucki or Sam Jones). He was a medicine man and a leader and had participated in all three of the Seminole Wars. He refused to leave his homelands. He was now the chief of about 250 to 300 remaining Seminoles.

Was Abiaka the sage I had been searching for?

THE MYSTICS AND THE MAGIC

In my mind's eye, he stands, tall and proud. He extends his arms out, across the land and up toward the sky. A supernatural energy expels from his extended fingers and the deed is done. Forevermore…

Who is this man, and does his magic still prevail? The supernatural powers of a sage may have been able to protect and guide current events of his time, but is it possible that a spell cast so long ago has the strength to continue to affect the present and the future?

Whenever a mystic or spiritual medium is witness to the residual magic of a sage, shaman, medicine man (*alektcas*), it is indeed a supernatural experience. The Seminole *alektcas* were able to magically transform what could have been toxic situations into sources of divine power and shields. The Seminoles believed that they were invincible under the strong leadership of their war chiefs and the protection of their spiritual *alektcas*.

Seminole fighters or guerrillas were legends of extreme and cunning fighting techniques. The term "guerrilla warfare" originated from and was savagely demonstrated during battle by these warriors. Some of the mystical chiefs, warriors and medicine men of the Seminole Wars included Micanopy, Jumper, Alligator, Abiaka, Abraham, Osuchee, Yaholooche and Billy Bowlegs.

The notable Abraham is directly connected to Sumter County history. Abraham was an escaped slave and founder of the African town of Abrahams Town or Pilaklikaha (also known as Palatlakaha, "Many Ponds" in the Mikasuki language) near where Center Hill now stands. He was known for his great skills of survival and negotiation. Earlier, before the Seminole Wars, he was one of the few that survived the "Negro Fort" (now Fort Gadsden) attack. Later, he was a leader and interpreter during the Second and Third Seminole Wars against the United States. After the Dade Battle, Pilaklikaha was destroyed by the army. Fortunately, Abraham and his villagers were able to escape weeks before the destruction of their home. Eventually, Abraham along with other Seminoles and Black Seminoles were forced to walk the Trail of Tears into what is now Oklahoma, where he died years later. His history lives on in the haunted Pilaklikaha settlement.

Recent historic discoveries at Old Abrahams Town involve archaeological finds. The site was once known as Pilaklikaha, a town inhabited by Abraham and other Black Seminole Indians during the early 1800s. The ghostly village remains were excavated recently by Terrance Weik from 1998 until 2001. Underneath the ruins were buried a remarkable collection of early European and Seminole artifacts, including remnants of pre-Columbian occupation. Recovered items include lithics, ceramics, glass beads, trade pipe fragments, bottle glass, brick, cut nails and other metal fragments. A village's legacy can live on through a discovered past.

Did another legendary name jump out from the listing of warriors? It all came flooding back to me. It had only been a few weeks since I had experienced the haunted cry of a fierce warrior echo down at Jumper Creek. Jumper's spirit wanted to be heard. Once again, spirits speak through mystical senses to bring history back to life. Jumper's legacy remains present. The warrior's legendary name remains strong among today's Seminoles.

One of the most enigmatic characters among the Cherokees is Abiaka. He was a legendary mystic whose magic and fortitude may still prevail. The U.S. Army prefers to forget the name of this cunning spiritual *alektca* and war chief. His medicine was known to kill the soldiers' horses, "ghost" the warriors among the battle fields and influence natural disasters. I hungered for any answers to my many questions about Abiaka's magic.

When stalled in research, I often Google a bunch of unrelated words together to see what will appear on the Internet. It's my game of searching intuitively for a person, place or idea that somehow incorporates all my meanderings into a singular thought. One just never knows what can be found. Most of the time, this exercise is the beginning of the turning point to receive whatever answers I am destined to find.

World prophesy searches can be quite entertaining and interesting to say the least. But there it was: Abiaka, the Mystic's Revelation, posted by the anonymous "Anointed Groove" (http://worldprophesy.blogspot.com/2015/01/abiaka-one-of-greatest-medicine-men-in.html). I knew in that moment that my mystic character had found me. Had he ever really left?

His name, Abiaka, is indeed connected to magic and the Seminoles. One interpretation of his name was "Binocular" because he could see afar. By using his mystical insight along with prayer, a black magical drink, the art of purification, guns and resolve, he was able to maintain his territory during chaotic times.

It has been reported by many that he was present as an *alektca* and eventual war chief during all three of the Seminole Wars. Afterward, he was the last standing chief when all others had been killed or forced to leave Florida after the final conflict. But he was *not* moving anywhere. He spent the rest of his days in his homeland of Florida. Some say that he lived until ninety, some say two hundred; others claim that he is still spiritually alive today.

His powers were unprecedented. He was able to use his medicine to stir Seminole warriors into a frenzy while keeping the enemy at bay. Soldiers' horses would die, tracking dogs refused to enter the native camps and many of the United States soldiers lived in direct fear of the mystic's wrath.

Abiaka's ghosting protection of the Seminoles goes far beyond a warrior's blessings for just one battle. It was reported that during several fights, the soldiers were often baffled by the sudden disappearance and escape of their trapped enemy. Familiar with the land, the Seminole fighters could easily hide under the roots of tall trees or submerge deep into the swampy waters. But the most incredible mystical feat was the natives' ability to disappear or vanish into thin air. It was often reported that after a skirmish, when the gun smoke cleared, no Seminoles were in sight. All or most had been cloaked from danger, perhaps by the great Abiaka's magic.

As my Sumter County research unfolded, an interesting insight into Abiaka's possible everlasting effects came to light. Wildwood's Baker family's citrus business, like that of many other farmers, had been ruined in the winter of 1894–95. A brutal freeze had left the current crop ruined, and the citrus trees were completely devastated. All the citrus farmers were either forced to leave or, like the Bakers, revamp their citrus business into cattle ranching or other crops in order to survive the damage.

Right there in print, in Mark Andrews's 1994 *Orlando Sentinel* article "Devastating Great Freeze of 1894–95," a miniscule "oh by the way" had simply stated that it was the worst freeze in Florida since the winter of 1835. This nugget of information was stored away, until I realized later that the Dade Battle had happened in the winter of 1835.

Details of the massacre recalled how the freezing soldiers had buttoned up their waistcoats against the bitter cold. Their ammunition boxes were hidden underneath. Surprised by the sudden attack, they were unable to access their ammo for a quick lock and load. They were rendered helpless for a while until they could reach the ammunition boxes. Some of the recent white settlers, in their acquisitions of the Seminole land, had also discovered numerous citrus trees among the thick forest. The orange groves were likely planted by the original indigenous tribes when the Spanish brought the citrus over from Europe.

Is it possible that Abiaka conjured an enduring winter's spell to protect the Seminoles, one that continues to propagate and negatively affect the citrus crop of today? Through the years, up until the present, freezes continue to threaten and destroy some of the crops. The land may indeed still be haunted by Abiaka's spell.

Many continue to hail Abiaka's ingenious abilities. Some believe that his healing powers and protection are still available to those in need. There was a recent account from an anonymous contemporary Seminole writer who suffered a full brain aneurysm but miraculously survived. He credits Abiaka. The writer had been working on a true account of the medicine man's life. "He is everywhere, and all around us. Maybe Sam Jones or Abiaka is not a person, but an entire concept?"

Even though the mystic Abiaka had physically passed away at the age of ninety in 1863, many believe that this *alektca*'s powers linger. His illuminating stature transcends supernatural forces to allow one to possibly believe, without seeing, that magic exists. The evidence shows that it is possible for the manifestations of the past to still be living today on the haunted Byway of Sumter County, Florida.

PART IV

ELEPHANTS, MOBSTERS, BANK ROBBERS AND A MONKEY

BYWAY STOPS

Did I just smell elephants?

...gangster activity...

Her arm was twisted...

...and no one was hurt...

BUSHNELL HISTORY BRIEFING

Bushnell, for such a small town, yields many prestigious sites, events and activities. The population barely tops three thousand, yet the town is home to the county seat, Florida's Fourth National Cemetery, Dade Battlefield State Park, the Kenny Dixon Sports Complex, the Sumter County Historical Society and more. The agriculture-rich town was named after railroad surveyor John W. Bushnell.

The Native Americans and others were the original occupants of this bountiful land. White settlers arrived sometime in the 1870s after the natives had been expelled. They found the rich soil ideal for agricultural opportunities. The community was established when the post office was open in 1885. The first church was built in 1886, and the city of Bushnell was incorporated in 1911. Bushnell has been the county seat since 1912. The impressive 1914 county courthouse still stands and operates as the cornerstone of the community and the county.

The people of Bushnell continue to strive for new opportunities while retaining their friendly, hometown charm. The enriching environment is showcased through several annual events: the reenactment of the Dade Battle inside the state park, the Veteran's Day Celebration at Florida National Cemetery and the fall festival.

The fall festival features a family fun day of games, contests, foods, dancing, music and performing arts. The highlight of the festival is the famous Greased Pig Contest!

MARTIN AND THE MEDIUM, DOWNTOWN BUSHNELL

The day that Martin Steele, local writer and Scenic Sumter Heritage Byway representative, volunteered to show us his hometown of Bushnell was quite an experience. It was a blistering day as Martin, Larry and I braved the weather and the ghosts in Bushnell. We started out by walking around the quaint downtown. As we peered into doors, looked on top of buildings and stood in the middle of the streets, my folder and notebook became filled with psychic meanderings.

The Sumter County Courthouse Complex is quite impressive.

I felt a choppiness to the inside layout of the structure. Several hidden small rooms. Mysterious twists and turns. Someone or somebody had accidentally been locked inside one of these hidden chambers.

We walked around the outside of the massive courthouse structures. We decided not to enter, given the security, and there was probably no one around to confirm the hidden rooms or admit that they may have been the one(s) "locked up." Martin informed us later that the jail was back part of the courthouse complex. But that wasn't exactly the trapped

Sumter County Courthouse complex. "Who got locked in?" *Martin Steele Collection.*

feeling I had experienced. It was a more professional feeling rather than one of a prisoner.

Historically, many early courthouses throughout the country were destroyed by fire because of the vulnerable wooden construction and heat source. Most county courthouses during the twentieth century were rebuilt with brick or limestone on the outside and safes on the inside to create a more fireproof facility. Thus, the hidden rooms or closets could be justified, but the twists and turns still seemed odd. I still feel a disjointed shift in the courthouse. Who was accidentally locked in? A workman? And how were the twists and turns related to the vision? Medium impressions can be abstract or literal. It's quite a conundrum and may never be settled. No worries, your secret is safe for now. We crossed the street and entered the main blocks of Bushnell.

Perhaps while the first vaqueros rode across the western plains of America, a precolonial English and American pioneering "Cracker" lifestyle was being born out in the bush of central Florida's wilds. And now, there standing before me, tucked away right in the middle of downtown Bushnell across the street from the Sumter County Courthouse, was an old Cracker cabin from long ago. I walked closer to carefully study the rustic historic charmer.

Intuitively, I noticed the exhausted farmer husband and his tired wife relaxing deep in their rockers on the wooden front porch. The couple were probably enjoying a sip of something. There was a batch of dirty but happy kids littering the front porch. Some were swinging and hanging on to the porch pillars. There in front of me was a spirited family relaxing in their Cracker home. How I love when history and haunts come together!

The origin of the term "Florida Cracker" is somewhat questionable. Some say that the cracking sound made by the whips used by the early cowboys or white settlers coined the phrase, while a few believe it is the use of cracked corn to make moonshine. Both items were a necessity for working and living on these lands.

In the 1800s, maybe much earlier, before Florida's statehood, a variety of rough riders collected, caught and drove wild cattle to provide food for many outside the bush. During the Civil War, cattle drives increased to keep up with the demand to feed the hungry soldiers on both sides. After the war, the free-roaming cowboys were mostly replaced by farming settlers.

After the Civil War, many settlers had no other place to go. When the southern soldiers returned home to their sharecropping or small farms, everything was gone. Much of the land and farms in Kentucky, the Carolinas and Georgia, to name a few, had been depleted of good soil and livestock. Desperate soldiers had ransacked and stolen livestock, equipment and wagons. Once the war was over, there was nothing left except despair.

The citrus business in Florida was growing, as were other opportunities to harvest many other types of fruits and vegetables. Many migrated to Florida for a brand-new start. The incoming settlers had little. They had to wheel and deal to scrape out a living. Many lived off the land while cultivating a productive farm or ranch. Many natural ingredients were readily available. Survival often included the making and trading of moonshine.

Rifles, guns and bullets were few. Most were taken or sold. The most important tool to the Florida Crackers was a whip—thick undergrowth could be cleared, wild cattle could be controlled and small animals such as squirrels

Cracker-style house in downtown Bushnell. *Courtesy of Larry Hollingsworth.*

could be snapped out of the trees to feed the hungry family. The crack of the whip represented survival to the new breed of settlers to the area.

Many were not used to the unbearable year-round humidity and heat or the continuous onslaught of mosquitos. The tiny wooden-frame Cracker-style home featured heart pine siding, a gabled tin roof and front and back porches. The steep roof allowed rain to be collected or run off during downpours. The two-sided porches provided proper air flow for natural air conditioning and the wooden siding, like moonshine ingredients, was easily attainable in the woods and waterways around them.

For a short time in history as compared to the Native Americans, the Cracker lifestyle prevailed in Florida. It has been said that the last cattle run passed by Wildwood and other areas around 1946. Cattle ranching has developed into a very lucrative business in the Sumter County, Florida area, especially after the final citrus freezes. Many of the backroads traveled on the Scenic Sumter Heritage Byway are thickly populated with livestock and their young. The free-roaming cowboy, like the Native American, is long gone, but the spirit of them lives on through haunted lands of Sumter County.

Did I just smell elephants? And then I felt it…a pesky monkey crawling all over me.

How odd was this? In the small town of Bushnell, massive animal smells and an agitated primate were all around me. Martin advised me that the Loomis Circus has been coming into town for many years and that one of its main events was the elephant show. He wasn't sure about the monkey, but then he asked if I had ever heard of the Florida International Teaching Zoo in Bushnell. I could see an annual circus visit into town, but a zoo in Bushnell? And not just any zoo, but the most experienced International Zoo in Florida!

Larry and I recently met the passionate Dr. Mark Wilson and his dedicated staff at the Florida International Teaching Zoo (FITZ) for a tour. Besides the public excursions, FITZ offers several unique educational opportunities for qualified students of all ages. The zoo is an accredited educational facility through the Zoological Association of America.

Dr. Wilson is deeply committed to his lifelong work with endangered species. FITZ's primary goal is to teach and educate the public to protect the animals and the environment.

A black jaguar, spotted hyenas and giant tortoises are among the many animals living at FITZ that you can visit up close and personal (or at least three to four feet away). Oh yes, then there is Hector. The resident African Patas monkey. Raised by hand, Hector has mastered communication skills and behavior. This clever imp has been instrumental in helping Dr. Wilson work with his lesser Patas primates.

Come, "walk on the wild side" of Bushnell's endangered kingdom. Further information and reservations can be found through www.floridazooschool.org.

The psychic renderings of a monkey crawling all over me are finally off my back.

HUNT AND GANT

A strong connection to gangster activity…

There were many strong medium impressions felt that day on our adventure around Bushnell. Sometimes I receive just tidbits of information, and then as the day progresses, more specific details emerge as the events unfold in my mind.

Right on the corner plaza of downtown Bushnell is currently the SunTrust Bank. As I was walking up to the historic building, I felt a strong connection to gangster activity. Every town, whether big or small, has some sort of notorious past. I soon found out that Bushnell and nearby Webster raised two of the most famous mobsters of our time.

According to Samuel Parish's 2008 account, recalled in *Central Florida's Most Notorious Gangsters: Alva Hunt and Hugh Gant*, the World War I veterans were changed by their combat experiences. When they returned home to Florida, job opportunities were slim. In addition, the everlasting effects of the war left them angry, broken and full of despair.

As the years passed, the nation's economic struggles, as well as their own, continued. Their interests in the automobile soon became an obsession. As their mechanical skills developed and became more refined, so did the drive to use their knowledge for illegal financial gain. It started as a simple automobile fencing operation and soon developed into an extremely successful car theft ring.

Early on, Gant was known for his master planning and Hunt for the execution. Rarely caught, the Hunt-Gant gang operations grew to be the largest and most prolific car thievery in Florida and other southern states. "Get Gant" had become the media's tagline to these Florida bad boys.

It was a natural transition into bank robbery. Given their brilliant execution and car thievery background, the robberies were well planned with ingenious escapes. They were arrested more than a few times, once in Sumter County, but pardons, legal mistakes, successful appeals and jail escapes freed them to continue their criminal activities.

The misadventures of the Hunt-Gant gang included a handful of bank robberies, numerous post office jobs and an assault and robbery related to kidnapping. Eventually, the law caught up with them, and serious time was served—Gant in Alcatraz, Leavenworth and Tallahassee Prisons and Hunt in Atlanta. When their sentences were completed, they returned to Sumter County to responsibly live and legally work for many more years.

Illinois may have Al Capone and Texas may have Bonnie and Clyde, but reformed Florida outlaws and patriots Alva Dewey Hunt and Hugh Archer Gant are immortalized within the pages of Samuel Parish's book and on the Scenic Sumter Heritage Byway in Sumter County.

"BONNIE AND CLYDE" IN BUSHNELL

Her arm was twisted…and no one was hurt.

Hunt and Gant never robbed a bank in Bushnell—maybe because there wasn't one. The gang operated during the mid- to late 1930s. In 1926, the local bank had closed. Another one wasn't opened for another twenty years. However, I had psychically witnessed a bank robbery in Bushnell. I was determined to confirm my impressions.

The main motivation to enter the criminal life, most convicts say, is money. Our couple, "Bonnie and Clyde" (pseudonyms), were no exception. Just like Hunt and Gant, they were financially strapped. The husband, seeing no other possibility, convinced his wife to rob banks, perhaps twisting her arm.

Florida National Cemetery. Duty…Honor…Country. *Courtesy of SSHB–Tangent Media.*

She had been a bank teller and he a part-time postal employee. They soon became partners in crime. The FBI said that the use of clever disguises made it difficult to identify the crafty crooks. Their crime spree took them across Florida and into Alabama from 2012 until 2013. A local Bushnell bank was indeed robbed by the notorious couple in the fall of 2013.

A true "Bonnie and Clyde" life of living on the lam. For eleven months, they were able to defy the law. Their profits were used to pay bills and gamble at casinos. Finally, the FBI got the break it needed. An all-points bulletin had been issued for the getaway car used during an earlier robbery. A toll plaza camera snapped the vehicle and its license plate, leading directly to their arrest. Plea bargains were made. "Bonnie and Clyde" are now serving time, separately. Luckily for them, there was no gangster-style shootout. In fact, during their crime spree, no one was hurt.

A day at Bushnell, in Sumter County, with writer and Scenic Sumter Heritage Bypass enthusiast Martin Steele certainly provided this spiritual medium with some of the spirited local history and events of the past, present and future.

Before departing the Bushnell area, I want to take a moment to appreciate and educate the weary veteran and other folks about the Florida National Cemetery in Bushnell. The first interment was in 1988, and this majestic site continues to provide our veterans an everlasting resting place of peace.

Duty…Honor…Country
…may they rest in peace

Bushnell's motto is "Committed to the Quality of Life." This city is a living testament to its big heart and opportunities for all those wishing to spend time here, now and forevermore.

DON'T FORGET WEBSTER!

There are times when we are forced to move on, never due to lack of interest but usually because of time. Just south of Bushnell is Webster. This charming town is worth the stop, *always* on a Monday!

Webster, like many other communities, was established in the 1850s by white settlers after the United States displaced the Native Americans. It was originally named Orange Home but was later renamed. The postal service had a similar town name, and the locals were left to find an immediate alternate one. The local postmaster, George F. Hayes, simply picked up the dictionary on his desk—Webster's Dictionary.

Once home to the "Cucumber Capital of the World" and the Parson Brown orange, this community, after many hard freezes, has evolved into a productive cattle agri-business. In addition, for the past fifty years or so, it has operated one of the largest markets in America. Every Monday, year-round, rain or shine, the Webster Flea Market covers more than forty acres, contains two thousand stalls and accommodates 1,200 vendors. With this crowd, my psychic antennas will need a fine tuning before and after walking through the crowd, especially if I travel with local writer Martin Steele.

It's time to depart from the lower part of Sumter County and head north on the Scenic Sumter Heritage Byway toward Lake Panasoffkee to Rutland. Will paranormal finds include supernatural swamp creatures and other unexpected oddities? Anything is possible on the backroads of Sumter County!

PART V

MONSTERS, GATORS AND PETE

BYWAY WATERWAYS

I feel him all around me…

My heart just dropped…it was Pete!

The native serenely canoed by…

NATURAL HISTORY AND WONDERS

A variety of natural wonders abounds in Sumter County, especially when following the Scenic Sumter Heritage Byway. Sparkling waters glimmer in the many lakes, swamps, rivers and waterways. Majestic oaks and stunning pines shade the road as the glistening sunlight filters through the treetops. There are about twenty-two park and recreational areas in Sumter County. Boating, bicycling, canoeing, hiking, swimming, hunting and fishing opportunities are easily found just a few miles outside the towns and cities.

Up until two hundred years ago, the land stood basically untouched. For thousands of years, the indigenous tribes roamed, occupied and honored the natural resources offered here. Fishing, hunting and minimal farming provided well for them. The bounties of the area and settlement opportunities brought in the outsiders. Along with them came disease, death and destruction. Eventually, most of the natives were driven away. Often by recognizing the mistakes of the past, the present occupants of Sumter County are led to protect not only the people's history but also the land and wildlife.

The Scenic Sumter Heritage Byway organization started as a Community Action Group in March 2009. It aligned with the Sumter County Chamber of Commerce with the specific goal of improving the southern entrance into Sumter County in order to enhance and honor the National Cemetery experience.

Through the many years of determination, dedication and the tenacious organization of advocacy and government groups, the southern entrance as well as other backroads of Sumter County have been designated "Scenic," thus creating the Scenic Sumter Heritage Byway. A nonprofit since 2014, the Byway organization continues to develop and enhance the opportunities and events offered among many communities, including Webster, Bushnell, Sumterville, Rutland, Lake Panasoffkee and more.

The beautiful waterways of Sumter County, Florida, can be explored in so many ways! *Courtesy of SSHB–Tangent Media.*

There are many interactive ways to enjoy this haven—air boat rides, animal interactions, antiquing, dining and drinking wine, just to name a few. Besides Florida International Teaching Zoo, Gatorworld Parks of Florida Inc. also provides a family-friendly interactive animal experience. This attraction affords hours of fun with a petting zoo, a visit to the warm and fuzzy hands-on "Bunny House" and "up close and personal" alligator encounters.

Airboat rides are especially enjoyable to all your senses. The educational and entertaining experience as you soar through the endless waterways of Sumter County is unforgettable. Tom and Jerry's Airboat Rides and Swamp Fever Airboat Adventures are local companies that swiftly guide you through the natural habitats and wildlife wonders, including alligators, hawks, birds and more. The airboat rides amp up many of your raw senses with the swampy smell, taste and feel of the wilderness. But be aware: beyond the murky waters may lurk a sinister supernatural thing or two.

The Green Swamp coils throughout the natural wonders of central Florida. Hiking, fishing, bicycling, hunting and nature watching are abundantly available among the more than fifty thousand acres of the Green Swamp Wilderness Preserve. Given the lush surroundings, alternate activities could perhaps entail the investigations of supernatural creatures such as Bigfoot, a swamp monster or a wild man. Whether fantasy or fact, the area is haunted with many paranormal possibilities. In fact, locals continue to warn people even today about a monster living in the bogs of the Green Swamp.

SUPERHERO STATUS

His strength is superhuman. He lives among the swamps, inhabiting and animating vegetable matter anywhere. Immortal, he easily morphs from one life form to another. Physical and mental attacks mean little to him. He can easily regrow any body parts and is able to transfer his consciousness into whatever living matter is available. He is one of the most powerful beings in the DC Comics series.

You may never had heard about him until now, but Swamp Thing does exist. Creator Len Wein imagined the elemental swamp monster character while riding a subway in Queens, New York. Queens is a long way from any swampland, but somehow Wein's vision of the bog superhero was clearly instilled in his mind. His design was then forever immortalized by artist Bernie Wrightson. Swamp Thing came alive!

The story is told of the botanist Dr. Alex Olsen from Louisiana. He was murdered by his assistant, Damian Ridge, by an intentionally set chemical explosion. Olsen dies, and his body is dumped by Ridge into a nearby swamp. Dr. Alex Olsen is reincarnated into a humanoid pile of living and breathing vegetable matter. He then rises up as the Avatar of the Green, known as Swamp Thing.

Villains, enemies and romances mark the many misadventures of this conservationist and monster champion of the swamp. Swamp Thing fights good and evil outside and within to save himself, humanity and the world. He travels around the globe to save those in need. The Green Swamp in central Florida smothers hundreds of square miles, including Sumter County. Is it possible that our own Swamp Thing or monster resides inside the Green Swamp? I am haunted by the possibilities.

RUTLAND ENCOUNTER

I had read and heard some of the recorded reports and stories of supernatural beings haunting the local area. In the fall of 2012, a driver saw a large, unidentifiable beast stalking wild boar outside Bushnell. Numerous scary accounts from campers and fishermen of day and nighttime sightings of a hairy, bipedal intruder in Green Swamp have been recorded quite often in the last few years. It could indeed be possible that Bigfoot, a Swamp Creature or a wild man still exists close to where I stood now in Rutland. Even before visiting the swamplands of Sumter County or knowing of the Green Swamp, I felt the presence of a Swamp Man or creature.

Rutland Park is a pet-friendly hiking, boating and picnicking area right off the side of the road in the upper-northwestern part of the Scenic Sumter Heritage Byway. I was traveling alone that day when I reached the

I felt him all around me…. Is a Swamp Creature hiding in the foliage? *Author's collection.*

park. I pulled over to stretch my legs and look around. It was a beautiful, warm and bright day. It felt so good to feel the sun directly on me as I left the air-conditioned truck. Suddenly, I felt it…there was something or someone there.

Tapping into psychic meanderings, I paused and gave myself time to just sit with my immediate surroundings. There was a boat launch and a small bridge nearby. Each led directly downstream into a tree-lined channel. I noticed a fisherman far down the river. No vehicles were there except for my own. There was a camper park right next to the site. Everything seemed so quiet and serene. Then the wind kicked up and started to dance among the trees.

I feel him all around me…

I sensed a kinship with this supernatural soul. Who was he? Did he need help, or perhaps he just wanted to be remembered? Was he possibly some kind of a green Swamp Thing or monster?

Printed materials such as books, articles and the like are a great way to present one's own paranormal findings. Photographs, however, rarely can be published showing an actual supernatural appearance. Ghosts and spirits rarely pause in full living color to allow one to snap their paranormal poise.

Intuitive examination of photographs later often brings to life what was supernaturally felt at the time of the experience. Unfortunately, the need to enhance the photograph in order to carefully study the moment captured usually reduces the pixel quality of the picture. Seeking paranormal clarity often results in the photo smears and fuzziness.

I know I captured my swamp man that day. I felt him all around me. I carry his picture in my phone. I am more than happy to show him off. "Look!" I exclaim. "Don't you see him?" I'll ask. Some see him right away and others don't. Funny how the response is still somewhat the same: "What the heck!" or "What the heck?"

His Chewbacca-like features are quite plain to me in the picture. His dark, deep-set eyes, dog-like wet nose and small, lined, pouting mouth are surrounded by massive reckless long hair encircling his head and protruding from his ears and chin. Large ears dominate each side of his face. His front left paw or hand appears to be curled around the bridge ramp's pole in the image. Or perhaps it's a friendly gesture, waving at me or trying to draw me closer toward him. Four of his fingers can be seen quite clearly. Two of them show his protruding claws. What can be seen of his chest is quite hairy too.

His large upper body is mingled among the lush tree greenery. It is difficult to tell if he is indeed green or merely morphing into the nature colors and supernatural energy around him. It's not easy being green and more difficult to be seen, if camouflaged among the foliage.

Unlike the 1987 fantasy/buddy movie *Harry and the Hendersons*, I did not have a physical encounter with him. There was no need, as in the film, to strap him to my truck. And as some paranormal pals do, he did not follow me home that day. I knew he was there, and hopefully he will come again.

Skeptic or believer, it makes no difference to me. But there was a real live wild creature living in the Green Swamp area that day. I felt him all around me.

THE HAUNTING OF GREEN SWAMP

The Green Swamp Wilderness Preserve courses throughout the many deep veins of Lake, Polk, Pasco and Sumter Counties. The landscape provides pine flatwoods, cypress domes and hardwood swamps—plenty of space for the deer, hog, turkey and wild man to roam and hide. The myth of a swamp monster came to life deep inside the marsh. The Haunting Legend of Green Swamp was recently revisited by staff member Kevin Spear in the October 31, 1991 edition of the *Orlando Sentinel*.

His name was Hu Tu-Mei. It has been more than forty-five years or so when this hardy seaman left his home in the Far East to seek his fortune as a seaman. He left behind his beloved wife, four handsome sons and three beautiful daughters in Taipei, Taiwan. His arduous journey from his homeland eventually landed him nearly nine thousand miles away on a mysterious island in the Green Swamp Devil's Creek area of Florida. Bleached armadillo bones and whining mosquitos still litter the slough. And some say that his eerie wails of terror still haunt the bogs of the Green Swamp.

It is a heart-wrenching tale of a sad man's journey into madness. He earned his living as a sailor voyaging the open oceans and seas to support his precious family in Taiwan. His journey had taken him far away to Florida's port of Tampa. It was after he disembarked from the freighter that his troubles began. As he was regaining his land legs, the sorrow of his distant family became too much for him. Hu Tu-Mei became quite homesick. He was overwhelmed and heartbroken. He felt that he would never see his family again. Despite the many efforts of others to comfort this troubled soul, he became more uneasy. He spoke little or no words outside his own native tongue. Agitated and completely confused, he soon became very violent.

The shipping company staff had no choice. Hu had become uncontrollable. This madman needed to be subdued and hospitalized. Hu Tu-Mei's enormous strength coupled with his delirium made it almost impossible to restrain him. It took eight muscular men to hold him down and handcuff him. He was finally transported to a nearby Tampa hospital. Hopefully he would find the help he needed.

Unable to properly communicate with the doctors or nurses, Hu felt more helpless than ever. Nothing could be found to relieve him medically or mentally. The foreigner was unable to overcome his profound homesickness and fears. The hospital felt like a prison. He was going completely mad. He surrendered to his insanity and abruptly left the hospital. He vanished.

He walked and walked, scrounging, hiding and living off the land. He had no idea where he was going or what he was going to do. No one knows exactly how long he aimlessly wandered until he reached shelter or food. He finally located an island cloaked by the tall and willowy saw grass of Devil's Creek, part of the Green Swamp network. Scared and hungry, maybe he thought it would be a good place to settle for a while. He soon learned to hunt and kill armadillos. Later, it was translated that he thought of them "as the little pigs that nobody wanted."

Hu Tu-Mei's escape had the police baffled. Locals including hunters and volunteers joined in. Everyone wanted to find the mad man Hu. The search went on for months, and Hu's whereabouts were still unknown. Given his irrational behavior, citizens were terrorized by the missing, deranged monster who was on the loose. The poor man had become more of a feared animal than a lost man, and the public demanded he be found and captured.

The locals' horror was further fueled by the reoccurring account of a group of lost hunters. The local men's sudden disappearance and reappearance from the Green Swamp was very mysterious. All the men were experienced scouts of the area; however, when found, they stumbled out, dazed, shaking, afraid, confused and babbling. No one knows exactly what happened to the hunters. Their zombie-like behavior was never talked about again.

Reports started to filter in from three surrounding counties, including Sumter, of several home burglaries. Most residences were in rural areas and usually reported that very little had been taken. The public was still frightened, and no one felt safe from the crazy mad man. Once a mobile home owner officially reported that cookies and cereal were missing after a break-in.

Besides stolen food and supplies, Hu was finding other ways to maintain his manic nomadic lifestyle. He managed to find and cook corn that was left by the game wardens to feed the wild turkeys. The smoke rising from his campfire as he roasted his fresh corn eventually gave away his location. Lawmen had finally found the illusive lunatic.

Taking all precautions, a posse carefully moved in and surrounded Hu's camp. By then, the locals and the law had coined the maniac foreigner the "Green Swamp Wild Man." Finally, this wild man might be caught!

Hu was described as "a scared and strong little rascal." When first approached, he felt attacked and turn and bit the state's game and freshwater fish commission officer. When he was finally restrained, the group carefully examined Hu to make sure he was okay. The poor man was filthy, caked with mud and covered with raw scratches and hundreds of welted mosquito bites. He was naked and afraid!

He was taken into custody and officially charged with the theft of the cookies and cereal stolen from the mobile home. He was immediately locked up in a tiny cell and soon refused to leave it. In an act of total surrender and humility, he surprisingly dropped to his knees and bowed down to the jailers so deeply that his head touched the floor.

Now that Hu was captured, everyone wanted to know more about the story of the Green Swamp Wild Man. A Taiwanese woman from Wildwood was able to serve as his interpreter. She soon shared that Hu feared he would be killed by the jailers. He frighteningly exclaimed, "They are going to kill me, and I will rather kill myself first." Alarmed and concerned, Hu Tu-Mei was carefully searched by the authorities for a knife or any other instrument that may cause him harm. Nothing was found. Two days after his arrest, Hu was able to loop a belt through the cell bars and hanged himself at the Sumter County Jail.

Among his few belongings was $330 of seaman's pay. The Sumter County sheriff sent the money, along with a letter of condolence, to the Chinese embassy. This offered very little comfort to his devoted family so far away. They would never see their adored husband and father again. Somehow, Hu Tu-Mei had become lost in his own madness and could never find his way back home.

Was Hu Tu-Mei the true monster of the Green Swamp? Suicide may have relieved the man's fears, but does he haunt and keep the local myth alive? It is said that the Green Swamp Wild Man sported huge feet and was swift as a deer. Fact or fiction, the haunting legend of Green Swamp lives on.

THE *SWAMP BROTHERS* MYSTERY

In the spring of 2011, the *Swamp Brothers* show debuted on the Discovery channel. Sumter County, just like my parents' Villages residence, at the time was home to Robbie and Stephen Keszey in Bushnell. The reality show followed the siblings' wildlife passion and antics. The Keszey brothers' show was advertised as an *Odd Couple*–like set of brothers who tried to capture snakes and other swamp creatures.

The reality television show partnered Robbie, the experienced and hardened capturer of snakes and the like, with his brother, Stephen, a former New York City bartender. Like me, Stephen freaks out whenever he is near a snake. Skittish Stephen, it was said, was more comfortable with lounge lizards than real ones. The idea of finding and seizing snakes makes my skin crawl. But the disjointed bromance and silliness seemed to hold the audience's attention while they enjoyed the natural beauty of the surrounding Sumter County area. It never dawned on me then that I, too, would someday be stepping over snakes on my own rural property with Larry in central Florida.

It all started innocently enough. Robbie, even as a young boy, had a real passion for Florida's reptiles and amphibians. "I would catch frogs and baby turtles and stuff them into my pockets. I drove my parents crazy!" he said. By the age of eight, he was handling snakes, and by thirteen, his passion had grown from a few pet snakes into breeding and handling them.

Stephen traveled a different road. A city boy, he followed the music publicity field and enjoyed years of bartending. Since their youth, the brothers were always arguing, bickering and pestering each other. For many years, they lived separate lives until Hollywood came knocking.

The surprise offer of the reality show would provide the brothers an opportunity of a lifetime and their chance to work together. Given their differences, the brothers' partnership seemed a bit odd, but Stephen seemed eager to confront and overcome his fears of snakes while learning the ropes to help Robbie with "Florida's largest reptile sanctuary and exotic reptile dealership."

The show's success unfortunately was short-lived. The televised programs only lasted until the fall of 2012, but the exploits of the Sumter County snake and critter business continued. Then real life got a little complicated for Robbie Keszey and his business dealings. Shortly after the series ended, one of the brothers, Robbie, along with his business partner, Robroy MacInnes, was convicted of conspiracy to traffic in state and federally protected reptiles. Court records detailed the illegal snake-smuggling activities that occurred across several states. Stephen was never indicted. Robbie's direct involvement was questionable. Retributions were paid and life moved on.

The Keszeys' critter work continued for them among the bogs of Bushnell in Sumter County, Florida. Their passion and care of reptile preservation was further established through Animal Crossings Inc. reptile farm.

The summer of 2018 drastically changed everything for Robbie and Stephen Keszey. According to the Sumter County Sheriff's Department, an intruder unlawfully entered the Keszeys' property, broke into a back window of the critter building, stole property and then set the place on fire. The intense heat and flames were merciless. Despite their efforts at containing the destruction, the arsonist's fire destroyed the dwelling, leaving forty-three dead alligators and crocodiles inside. The brothers were devastated. Most of those killed were juveniles, but these precious reptiles were like family to the distraught owners. It was a blow to their business as well as a shot directly to their hearts.

Then the situation went from bad to worse. During the commotion, a rare white two-year-old Leucistic alligator named Snowball went missing. The brothers and others searched frantically for the missing alligator. It soon became apparent that perhaps Snowball had been stolen. The gator's kidnapping may have been the motivation for the arson. The priceless white alligator with blue eyes is quite unusual and worth well over $100,000.

The Sumter County Sheriff's Office, Crimeline and Gatorland partnered to offer a $7,500 reward for the return of Snowball. Robbie's biggest fear is that Snowball will never be found. "The hope is they can find Snowball before he's smuggled out of the country or becomes part of a private collection."

Robbie Keszey estimated his total losses, including Snowball's disappearance, at between $150,000 and $200,000. He has raised animals at his farm for more than twenty years and doesn't know where he will go from here. Will Snowball ever be located? And who maliciously destroyed Animal Crossings' compound building, alligators and crocodiles?

Robbie and Stephen Keszey are still severely affected by the cruel and intentional act. The land and peoples of Sumter County, Florida, like Swamp Brothers Robbie and Stephen Keszey, are haunted by their losses. Hopefully someday the answers will be found. This is still an ongoing investigation. If you have any information, please do not hesitate to contact the Sumter County's Sheriff Department.

JOURNEY'S END AT THE PANA VISTA LODGE

The native serenely canoed by…

Our paranormal journey continues down the Scenic Sumter Heritage Byway. Sometimes when traveling, when you least expect it, something or someone from your past finds you—a haunted memory comes back to life, a gentle reminder of what was and what will never be again.

A while back, I visited the Pana Vista Lodge at Lake Panasoffkee. I know I was led there. Two lasting visions played out during my visit to the lodge and fishing camp, and of course, I found a monster. Until that time, I was unfamiliar with the Lake Panasoffkee regional history.

Lake Panasoffkee, or "Valley of Water" (conceivably named from the Mikasuki language) was once home to the early Native Americans. Boggy Island was settled by Central African slaves from the Kongo, and neighborly Black Seminoles settled in nearby Sitarkey's Village around 1813. Indian Mound Springs and Gum Slough were close by in this fertile valley. The

Black Seminoles raised cattle, horses and hogs and grew corn, rice and sugar cane. It was also said that they planted and nurtured one of the oldest and finest orange groves in Florida.

The Lake Panasoffkee region was used by the Seminoles for tribal councils and Green Corn Dances. It was and remains a very sacred place, some say. Perhaps Abiaka's magical power of protection extended into this region. For whatever reason, Sitarkey's Village was untouched during the Second Seminole War. It provided a haven for many Seminole families during the war.

Twice the village was visited by the U.S. Army looking for Seminole warriors. It wasn't until 1837 that the village was unexpectedly raided. Fifty warriors and their families barely escaped their gruesome fates. Just a few were captured. Nonetheless, the village was no more.

The citrus grove was soon being farmed by white settlers. The damaging freezes of the 1880s and 1890s wiped out the citrus industry, and most of the farmers were forced out of the former native village. Many believe that the great medicine man Abiaka and his cloaking spell hid most of the Seminoles from the soldiers' sight. Perhaps the sage's powerful magic still protects the sacred haunted village and land today.

Eventually, Charles G. King, a land developer from Cleveland, bought 2,500 acres in Lake Panasoffkee and developed the Monarch Orange Grove in 1908. In 1926, the citrus orchard produced more than forty thousand boxes of prime oranges. Other sections of the lake area were developed for a variety of uses.

On the premises of what is now the Pana Vista Lodge was a citrus packaging plant called the Panasoffkee Packing Company from 1885 to 1912. A few years earlier, a large plantation home had been built on the Outlet River in the 1880s by the Harris family. The wife was the daughter of the prominent White Sewing Machine Company family. She had no desire to live in the swampy, humid Florida country. The large home was soon sold to the King family. Plans were made for a tuberculosis sanitarium. These plans never materialized.

The property was then sold in 1923 to Mr. and Mrs. W.M. Knight. The residence was expanded and remodeled and soon began operations as a successful hotel. Many tourists from the North wintered there and enjoyed hunting and fishing on the nearby land. In 1929, the hotel burned to the ground.

The Savage family bought the property from the Knights sometime in the mid-1930s. The fishing and hunting camp expanded with the addition of a few cabins. Then the real estate was sold to Sid and Bessie Lee in the early 1940s. Mr. and Mrs. John Veal and Mr. and Mrs. Rufus Wyson bought the lodge and formed a partnership in 1948. Sadly, John Veal died in 1951, and surprisingly, the Veal family purchased the property from the Wysons.

The determined widow Elizabeth Veal was soon joined by her son, Jim Veal Sr., and his family. The second generation moved from northwestern George to help Elizabeth manage the popular camp. Jim Veal Jr. started working full-time to join on as the third generation to own and operate the family facility. His daughters, as the fourth generation, have been instrumental in keeping the busy camp running smoothly as well.

The trip off the main highway to the Pana Vista Lodge is quite quaint. Scattered small lake homes and cabins are lined up with mobile homes along the backroad. Right away, an old-fashioned feeling encases you as you enter the property. It is a full-service fish camp, including live bait, a tackle shop, cabins, a campground and boat rentals. The campground spaces include room for tents and RVs—a one-stop shop for all your fishing needs.

As I drove up and climbed down from the truck, the most unexpected visitor greeted me on the front covered porch. He took my breath away for a moment.

My heart just dropped…it was Pete!

The black crooked cat with the red-tinged highlights on the ends of his hair looked up at me, and I lost it. Pete!

The way the feline contorted its every move, breathed its soft *meow* and looked at me with those clear, knowledgeable eyes, for a moment of time my sweet Snowball Pete had come back to life! He had lived for nearly nineteen years, and his passing had left me lost for quite some time. His spirit was clearly standing in front of me, but in this case, her name was Inky. What a ghostly warm welcome to the Pana Vista Lodge.

The camp's office and store are very homey. The wooden cabin-like structure is rustic, charming and efficiently cluttered with all types of memorabilia and goods for sale. Every space on the walls is covered with every imaginable item possible. One could spend days just walking around, looking. I spoke to the owner, Jim, as well as campers and a friend or two. The story is common here: "I came as I kid and now, I bring my own kids… or grandkids." Warm and fuzzy feelings are felt all around.

Store patron Dale Edwards poses with author and one of many local lake oddities on display. *Photo by Jeannie.*

I was noting some of the more interesting items and was drawn to a Swamp Monster's head mounted on the wall. This one seemed smaller, more like a creature—perhaps even a man-made animal with interestingly odd features. Photographs were taken, and then I headed outside.

The water was calling to me. The spirit of Pete was still leaving me a bit unsettled. I wandered out to the dock and sat down on a comfortable wooden bench. It was so quiet and peaceful. The water was barely rippling at the dock, and then I saw him—the native serenely canoeing by. He was paddling his canoe precisely, cutting through the smooth water as he peacefully glided by me. I was mesmerized. He was tall, dark, almost majestic, and his muscular body easily navigated the craft. His black hair hung down, with a few hawk feathers streaming down from his long locks. The sun danced on the smooth waters as he cruised by. My eyes followed him down the waterway until he was out of sight. I, too, believe that this is a sacred place.

The native serenely canoed by.... The Pana Vista Lodge. *Author's collection.*

There are other fish and camping grounds nearby, such as Idlewild Lodge and RV Park, Big Cypress Fish Camp, Watson's Resort and Fish Camp, just to name a few. Each is unique. I invite you to explore them. For some reason, I was led to the Pana Vista Lodge. Unexpected treasures from the beyond are always appreciated. To see and greet my dear Snowball Pete again, down to his red-tinged hair, was a gift. Pete's heart was pure, and he was a great warrior. His spirit spoke to me, and my heart sank with sadness and love.

The mounted marsh creature at the Pana Vista Lodge was not exactly my vision of the Green Swamp man I saw. I think mine looked more like the spirited DC Comics superhero Swamp Thing. Hopefully I will find out someday and be able to commune with him again.

As the Native American spirit floated away, I wondered if Abiaka's magic had reached out and ghosted this Seminole warrior and his family from harm's way. And now this brave's heart, like Pete's, lives on within the haunted lands and waterways of Lake Panasoffkee, on the sacred Scenic Sumter Heritage Byway in Sumter County.

PART VI
LOST SOUL AND UNSOLVED MURDERS

BEFORE LEAVING THE BYWAY

I heard the crying again.... There was a connection...

CONTACT

That day in the Lake Panasoffkee area had been filled with unexpected psychic connections. As I walked back to the truck, I relaxed and started to chuckle about the fun I had with the Pana Vista Lodge staff, posing with the mounted creature and admiring the odd assortment of items throughout the camp store. As I started the truck, I took a last look back. I knew I would return. But for now, I was exhausted. And yet I still felt a lingering energy. Sadness and a sense of being lost haunted me. I tried to shake off the undetermined feeling. It was best if I headed home. A good meal and night's rest would help me calm down. As I turned onto the highway, an uneasiness continued to surround me.

I then remembered that amid all the other psychic energy detractions, I *had* heard the sound earlier in the day. It was when I was entering the Lake Panasoffkee area. I had been thinking ahead to the visit and not listening to my medium impressions. Weary and concerned, I wondered why she was weeping. Why now, why here and what was she trying to say?

On my way home, I replayed the eventful Sunday morning when I had first heard the weeping. Larry had chauffeured that day. Good thing, too, since I was practically driven mad trying to locate the source of the wail. It was a special day, as I had experienced the familiar mother-and-child communion with the spirits at the Nichols Family Cemetery and my own mom. And now the crying had returned.

When first investigating for a project, besides searching out psychically, I often look for connections and ideas by talking with others, walking up and down the aisles of local libraries, roaming backroads, attending meetings and listening to the locals. At the Scenic Sumter Heritage Byway meeting, there was a brief mention of an unsolved murder, or murders, in the Sumter County area involving Oak Grove Cemetery. I had filed the information aside at least temporarily because, well, I was nervous.

I had been asked to do a presentation in front of the Byway organization, and even though I have presented many times, it still gives me butterflies in my stomach. My preparations paid off though, as the talk went very well. The group was receptive. I left, eager and all charged up with all kinds of ideas floating in my head—one of those being the mysterious Oak Grove Cemetery mystery.

I admit I did a little Oak Grove crime investigating on my own, noting tidbits, picking up articles and printing off areas to explore later. But then the overwhelming task of writing the book took over. I put the research away for future reference for future chapters in the book. Now it seems my visit to Lake Panasoffkee had brought the information front and center.

The first physical contact with her dead body was on February 19, 1971. Teenage hitchhikers had found the poor darling submerged in the black acidic waters beneath a highway overpass in Lake Panasoffkee off Interstate 75. That was near the same vicinity where I had heard the weeping a second time.

DISCOVERIES

The Sumter County Sheriff's Department immediately started its thorough investigation of the female victim's death. An autopsy was ordered. The sheriff's department released information as quickly as possible. No documented identification had been found on her. They were determined to find out who this Jane Doe was and what maniac may have killed her. The sheriff's office, from the very beginning, investigated the murder case with a fierce doggedness.

A thorough forensic examination of the young lady was conducted by Dr. William Schutze. The report stated that a man's size-36 belt had been found wrapped tightly around her throat—death by homicide by ligature strangulation. A rib had been fractured during the murderous act. More than likely this was caused when the perpetrator was holding her down while he killed her. Or perhaps the break occurred if her body had been tossed from the Lake Panasoffkee bridge. The evidence also indicated that she had been dead for three to four weeks before her body was found by the hitchhikers.

The unknown victim was a young woman between the age of seventeen and the mid-twenties, between five-foot-two and five-foot-five and at death weighed between 110 and 120 pounds. It was further noted that she'd suffered malnutrition or some sort of disease or illness when young that had stunted her growth. Long dark hair and brown eyes with high cheekbones suggested that she had European or Native American ancestry.

The Sumter County's Sheriff's Department went to work. In addition to the autopsy, it carefully collected, recorded, examined and photographed Jane Doe's sparse possessions and clothing. The young woman was dressed in a green shirt, green plaid pants and a green floral poncho. She also had a white gold Baylor wristwatch, a gold necklace and a gold ring on her ring finger. The ring was set with a transparent stone. It is believed that the woman may have been married. The postmortem examination indicated that she appeared right-handed and had given birth to at least two children.

As I read through the many reports and media stories, grief for this lost soul overwhelmed me. The mother-and-child reunion, or separation, was heart-wrenching. My mind was spinning. Often when psychic messages come through, there is more than one reason, and I realized that I, just like Sumter County Sheriff's Department and the public, wanted justice and peace for this poor unidentified mother.

Six months into the murder investigation, it came to a dead stop. No clues, no family coming forward and no suspect in sight. Sadly, despite the best efforts of the law enforcement agencies, media and public, no one stepped up to identify the young woman or her killer. Gone but not forgotten, the community's Jane Doe darling was laid to rest at

Oak Grove Cemetery. Almost fifty years later, it is the same cemetery I accidentally stumbled across on my way to Royal while following my medium impressions.

NEW FINDINGS

In 1986, Sheriff Jamie Adams had the cold case reopened. Despite the endless efforts of the public, media and law enforcement agencies, no one stepped up to identify the young woman. It was difficult for the compassionate Floridians, especially Sheriff Adams, to keep the victim the anonymous Jane Doe. A nickname formed from where she was found and because of her small statue, and she was soon affectionately called "Little Miss Lake Panasoffkee" or "Little Miss Panasoffkee." With the case now reopened, advanced forensic medicine discovered and innovated over the years has shed more light on the young woman's murder. An anthropologist discovered that the "Watson-Jones" orthopedic surgery had been performed on her right ankle when she was about sixteen years old. Then the sheriff contacted a forensic artist to use her expertise to re-create a more detailed composite sketch of the young victim based on her human skeletal remains.

The artist used X-rays and photographs of the woman's skull in order to update her previous image. A new technique of age regression was used to show how the victim may have looked from childhood until her death. Flyers were created and distributed throughout the country including law enforcement agencies. Unfortunately, despite these endeavors, no new clues emerged to break the cold case.

In the early 1990s, the Little Miss Lake Panasoffkee cold case was featured on the television series *Unsolved Mysteries* and then later *Cold Case Files*. It was said that the victim could have been a runaway and had only been in the United States less than a year, perhaps even one to three months prior to her murder. Even though further details clearly indicated that she had once been well nurtured because of the professional care extended to her dental and medical needs, no loved one came forward and no real new evidence was reported after the shows aired.

GREAT EXPECTATIONS

There she lies, unknown, in her grave, all alone at Oak Grove Cemetery. The Sumter County Sheriff's Department has not forgotten her though. Science continues to become more sophisticated, and in 2012, a new analysis indicated that she was of Greek origin, perhaps the Lavrion region based on her dental testing. Her story was soon featured on a Greek missing persons' show.

Finally, a break in the case came through from the televised show in Greece. A viewer called in and identified the victim as a possible former school friend of hers, Konstantina. The two girls had attended school together in Kifisia, a suburb of Athens. The girls, along with other female students, were part of a school program that sent the young ladies out after training to either Australia or the United States. The viewer had lost touch with her friend when each was sent to separate countries. Apparently, Konstantina and two other girls had been sent to the United States. The viewer had lost touch with her fellow student and friend and was willing to help find her now. Perhaps Sumter County's young Little Miss Lake Panasoffkee had finally been identified.

However, the possibility was short-lived. A caller that identified herself as one of Konstantina's daughters had seen the updated show and reported that her mother was not missing. Her mother was indeed alive and had, in fact, been sent to Australia as a young girl. Then the plot thickened. A new twist came into play when the "daughter's" call never resulted in any relatives of Konstantina stepping forward nor being located. It was as though her daughter, like her, had vanished into anonymity and would never be found again.

Around the same time that the Greek connection was being worked, a stateside Greek community in Tampa Bay of Tarpon Springs was being investigated for possible answers. It was less than a two-hour drive away down I-75, so a killer could have easily left the Tarpon Springs area and dumped the victim. Despite the six thousand pamphlets distributed to the residents and businesses in the Greek community and the heavy law enforcement involvement, once again no new leads were developed.

Even though it has been nearly fifty years, Little Miss Lake Panasoffkee's unsolved murder has never been forgotten by the Sumter County community. The Sumter County Sheriff's Department remains committed to solving this case. It wants to bring justice and a proper name to the murder victim. The young lady's DNA is on file in case someone, someday, steps up and claims her as family or admits to her vicious killing. Eternally, she waits at Oak Grove Cemetery.

Little Miss Lake Panasoffkee is haunted by her own identity.

This is an ongoing cold case in Sumter County, Florida. Anyone with any possible information, please contact Lieutenant Jon Galvin at the Sumter County Sheriff's Office (352) 569-1600.

KINSHIP TO DEATH

There was a connection…

They were young misguided lovers—strangers, really. She was Shirley Elizabeth Whitten and he was Roger Dale Higgins. On February 22, 1972, their gruesome fate would find them together brutally stabbed to death in a remote part of Oak Grove Cemetery outside Wildwood in Sumter County, Florida.

Just barely nineteen years old, Whitten, a Coleman resident, worked as a clerk at the Union 76 truck stop in Wildwood. Higgins, twenty-six, had stopped at the Union 76 station with his employer to rest. The Sumter County Sheriff's Department carefully retraced each victim's life and specific steps that day to help locate their killer.

It was very early in the morning that day when the altercation took place. The crime scene indicates that someone had apparently followed them into the cemetery and, in a rage, killed her and then him. According to the investigator, Major Gary Brannen, "Their deaths are believed to be the work of one man, someone who knew Whitten and became provoked because of her involvement with Higgins."

The couple had planned to drive out to a remote area early that morning to have sex. It is not clear how well each victim knew the other until that day. It is believed that the jealous suspect had seen the two together or perhaps asked about Whitten's whereabouts. Either way, the assailant may have decided to follow them and perhaps planned to confront the duo at the remote cemetery location.

It isn't exactly known when the suspect arrived or how long he waited. Perhaps his original plans never included murder. The perpetrator's weapon had been a simple pocketknife. Either way, he did indeed approach them. Brannen believes that "the suspect was probably jealous…in a rage," he said. "He slashed the car tires and then things escalated from there."

The crime scene clearly spoke of a coldblooded act. Their bloodied bodies were found next to each other. She was half clothed, and he had been dragged back from the car; both were covered with numerous stab wounds. Each cut was no larger than one centimeter in width. Each stab left less than a half-inch mark. Each of them had been repeatedly knifed close to thirty times or more.

Their maimed bodies were found about five hours later by a man who had come into the cemetery to repair a broken headstone. The visitor was shocked by the terrible scene he had stumbled across. He immediately called

Oak Grove Cemetery leads into several murder mysteries. *Author's collection.*

A lost soul. "Little Miss Lake Panasoffkee" is haunted by her own identity. *Author's collection.*

and reported about the dead bodies lying together outside a 1969 Chevrolet. It was the same vehicle the twosome had driven from the Union 76 truck stop to the Oak Grove Cemetery.

These murders are not believed to have been random killings or the work of a serial killer, but rather a simple act of one madman's rage. No one has ever been arrested. No suspect has been found. It is still believed that this unsolved murder can be solved. "Somebody local knows about this case and they could help solve this case," stated Brannen. And now it has been close to fifty years ago.

While I was deep in research and collecting data for the Little Miss Lake Panasoffkee cold case, did I accidentally find and slip in the printout of the Lovers' Enraged Killer one too? Was there some time of connection to each of the unsolved murders? Or simply random similar acts that could somehow connect the dots that aren't there? I know, here I go on with the ramblings of a spiritual medium who psychically records the "what ifs" in the random ways of patterns in energy.

But let's carefully examine the similarities. Little Miss Panasoffkee's body was found on February 19, 1971, and the couple's murder was on February 22, 1972. She was buried at Oak Grove Cemetery six months after she was found. The twosome was stabbed to death at Oak Grove Cemetery a year later very close to the same date of when the young woman was found.

All of them had been savagely killed—perhaps the work of a jealous assailant. It was stated that Little Miss Panasoffkee had been well kept because of her medical and dental work, and perhaps both women knew who had viciously attacked and murdered them. There had to be some type of connection.

Little Miss Lake Panasoffkee is never far from my mind, and apparently, as bizarre as it seems, this other Oak Grove Cemetery cold case may be somewhat related. Was her mysterious death the cause of a young couple's death about a year later? Could the killer of Little Miss Lake Panasoffkee have created and continued his crazed obsession with her? Did his adoration of her extend past her death? Is it possible that perhaps the young lady's attacker was visiting her grave and was taken aback by the unsavory behavior of the young lovers? Were they, in his mind, desecrating her sacred final resting place? Could he, in his madness, have stabbed the unsuspecting lovers to death? Or were the ladies both familiar with their attackers? The dates, the place and the motive are a bit far-fetched—at least for the moment.

Both cases remain unsolved. Close to fifty years ago, a killer or two ended the lives of three young people. They were loved and they had dreams, and somehow they lost their lives near or on the Scenic Sumter Heritage Byway.

Anyone with any possible information, please contact the Sumter County Sheriff's Office at (352) 569-1600.

CONCLUSION

T hank you for reading *Haunted Sumter County, Florida*! It was certainly a lot of fun for me to learn about the history and haunts on and near the Scenic Sumter Heritage Byway and, most importantly, to have you join me. You're now ready to relive or discover the paranormal possibilities on your own. Perhaps even solve a mystery or two! Many activities, tours, attractions, parks and events mentioned are right outside your door. Before you jump into your car or turn another page, be sure to include some delicious stops for wine, chocolate and beer.

Sumter County has two spectacular countryside winery choices and a huge chocolate supermarket, offering you some armchair goodies before you travel any further. It seems only fair to mention them since my love of chocolate and wine are equal to my passion for the paranormal. Visit Russell Stover Chocolates to sample the ice cream and load up on the old-fashioned fudge, caramel apples and fine chocolates. Pair the edible delights with some blueberry wine or beer from Whispering Oaks Winery or sixty-four-ounce growlers and wine "to go" from the Backyard Barn Winery and Microbrewery.

While shopping, sipping, licking or chewing your delights, look around and ask, "Is this place haunted? Or are these yummy delights just out of this world?"

I challenge you to get out there and investigate the past, present and the paranormal. Don't be surprised if Larry and I are standing there enjoying a sundae or some blueberry beer while waiting for an airboat ride after visiting the gators. The journey is never over. New supernatural discoveries are made every day when you travel the psychic avenues near or on the Scenic Sumter Heritage Byway in haunted Sumter County, Florida. Turn off your GPS and go!

EPILOGUE

How exactly do people perceive ghosts? Can you believe that we are born with the ability? Have you ever observed how a young baby may unexpectedly stare and start interacting with what seems to be just an empty space across the room? Giggling, he will reach out, thrusting his chubby arms and hands toward something or someone that isn't there. Laughing and wiggling, he seems to be communicating with someone. An older child sometimes talks about speaking and visiting with nana, even though the child's grandmother had died before the child was born. A good nana never loses touch with her loved ones, even from the spirit world.

Other interactions with the spirit world may be the sensation of someone sitting and sinking into your bed or seeing a reflection of a stranger in a mirror who turns out to be a deceased child. As mature adults, the idea of communicating with the dead becomes surreal for most. By this time, many have dismissed the idea that talking to the dead is possible.

Knowing that such communication is possible, how do you know when a ghost is around? Changes in the energy encircling you often indicate the presence of a ghost. A chilly sensation, with goosebumps running up and down our arms and legs, is one of the most common reactions to an unexpected surge. The smell of freshly baked peanut butter cookies at nana's old house, an unexplained knocking on the wall, an acidic taste in your mouth or a mysterious light flying around the room and disappearing into the wall—interactions with ghosts are possible. Your senses are vital tools, especially your sixth sense, to open the lines of communication with ghosts.

Is it possible to go beyond one's own senses and learn to witness spirits? Many who believe in ghosts feel that Heaven, or the Other Side, is simply a breath away. By lifting the veil that separates life from death, one can experience the manifestation of a ghostly interaction.

The idea of spirits is very comfortable and comforting to me. As a child, I had tea parties with them. I carried them in my little red wagon. I helped bring them comfort. As I grew older, so did my own training, education and experience with the spirit world. I learned to sit with them and be one with the other side. The technique I use can easily be put into play if you want to try to have your own ghostly experience.

The presence of ghosts has been recorded and talked about since the beginning of time. Spirits are known to haunt cemeteries, castles, homes, businesses, people and, as represented in this book, the haunted land of Sumter County, Florida. How do you know when something or somewhere is haunted?

There are often stories, legends, myths and previous experiences of others that foretell of a haunted location. The Dade Battlefield spirits have been experienced and recorded by many through the years. Numerous stories have been passed down through the generations for years or from experiences today of hearing the ghostly echo of the cannons and gunfire, as well as the ascending of the spirits from the battlefield during the battle reenactment.

On my first visit to a location or site, I prefer to know nothing of the ghost stories, legends or history. Simply picking or being led to a place and planning the visit with no or little prior knowledge is my first step. By using my own sixth sense, I open myself up to the possibilities. Once recorded, I then research and compare my own medium impressions to what others have recorded in history or their own personal accounts—like with the case of the beautiful Baker House in Wildwood and Laurence's big fish ghost story. The docents knew of his death and some visitors had sensed a little boy, but did they know of his own eagerness to share his big fish encounter?

Allowing one's own mind to transcend time and place can provide an opportunity to experience the haunted history of Sumter County or anywhere else. Let's take a moment to cover a few of the ghost hunting basics that you may be able to use and find out firsthand if a place is haunted.

I know you've watched the television shows. Fancy equipment such as tape recorders, EVP and ghost boxes, infrared lights, night-vision cameras, EMF Meters, K2 Meters, Mel Meters, you get the idea. They all seem necessary for your ghost hunting needs.

I'll let you in on a little secret. The best set of equipment is free! It is what lies right between your psychic ears: your own intuitive mind. We are all born with a sixth sense. By tapping into our natural ability, the opportunity to sense, speak and experience with spirits can be quite rewarding. Learning to tune in to the spirit world can be very simple.

Equipment is as easy as going to your local store. A notebook, a pen, a phone (serves as camera, recorder and phone) and chocolate are all you need. A flashlight, water and proper clothing, including sturdy footwear, are recommended too. Don't forget a first-aid kit. Now that you're equipped, plan on your ghost hunting party and the location.

It's better to not go alone. The buddy program is recommended with the living or the dead. Safety in numbers is important for keeping up with one's whereabouts. However, for the best results, I recommend once you arrive at the site or location to divide up in a group of no more than two. This allows each person to develop and learn their own technique to commune with the supernatural energies around them. And it's always fun to compare what others have experienced. It is uncanny how psychic impressions and sensations are many times the same.

Sensing ghosts is a matter of allowing at least one of our five basic senses—sight, hearing, smell, taste and touch—to interact with the spirited energy around us. The other side is around us all the time. It is simply the technique of tuning in, being quiet and allowing the spirits to speak.

Location and time of day don't really matter. Be sure to respect the rules of where you plan to ghost hunt. Plan a site with the understanding that while driving there you may be psychically led to an alternate location. Just take off and stop when you feel a different energy and then continue if time allows to your original location.

Cemeteries are one of my favorite locations. The quieter the better, especially if you are a novice spirit seeker. Just pick a spot and sit down with notebook and pencil in hand (look out for ant hills!). Let your mind and senses be open. Without hesitation, write down whatever you are receiving. Smells, numbers, coldness, whispers…don't discount anything you are receiving.

At the same time, be open to when you are led to record or photograph what is going on around you. Recording sessions are simply having a conversation with a ghost. Is there a ghost here? What do you want to say? Be sure to leave plenty of silence between questions to allow the spirits the opportunity to speak. By listening later, you may be surprised with your results. A voice, a bang, a laugh or a cry are just a few of the recordings I have heard.

Along with the recording ability, most phones are quite sophisticated now and can take some high-quality pictures. When inclined to do so, snap away. I recommend a series of three photographs. If a spirit's presence is there, the orb, wisp or embodiment will last just a moment. The before-and-after photographs help you determine if an unknown energy was present. Also be sure to download the pictures later and carefully examine them. Often manifestations and visions are larger or smaller than expected. Be open to any possibilities.

Once the ghost session is completed, join the others in the group and talk about what each experienced, recorded or photographed. Commonalities are often confirmation enough of a ghostly encounter. When time allows, checking the history compared to the experience can be quite astounding. Sometimes I would have a group member volunteer to do the history before the event and then share at the end. Please keep in mind that messages received may be historical or meaningful to you or someone else in your group or family.

So, what happened? Did you sense an older male? A happy dog? A disjointed feeling or a sour taste? Was a message given to you? Never discount what has been recorded and keep an investigation journal. Later answers to your impressions may come to light. Don't get discouraged, especially the first time or two. Ghost investigation and communication is a trained practice.

Often people ask, "How do you know if something or somewhere is haunted?" My favorite answer is: I don't know until I've experienced it myself. And that is how *Haunted Sumter County, Florida* came to be.

BIBLIOGRAPHY

Allman, T.D. *Finding Florida: The True History of the Sunshine State*. New York: Atlantic Monthly Press, 2013.

Brown, Robin C. *Florida's First People*. Sarasota, FL: Pineapple Press Inc., 2007.

Cerulean, Susan. *"Restorying Florida": The Wild Heart of Florida*. Gainesville: University Press of Florida, 1999.

DeLorme. *Florida Atlas & Gazetteer*. Yarmouth, ME, 2010.

De Wire, Elinor. *The Florida Night Sky*. Sarasota, FL: Pineapple Press, 2002.

Gannon, Michael. *Florida: A Short History*. Gainesville: University Press of Florida, 2003.

———. *The New History of Florida*. Gainesville: University Press of Florida, 2000.

Gordan, Elsbeth. *Heart and Soul of Florida: Sacred Sites & Historic Architecture*. Gainesville: University Press of Florida, 2013.

Hunt, Bruce. *Visiting Small-Town Florida*. 3rd ed. Sarasota, FL: Pineapple Press, 2011.

Jenkins, Greg. *Chronicles of the Strange and Uncanny in Florida*. Sarasota, FL: Pineapple Press, 2010.

Jones, Maxine D., and Kevin M. McCarthy. *African Americans in Florida*. Sarasota, FL: Pineapple Press, 1993.

Kabat-Zinn, Jon. *Wherever You Go There You Are*. New York: Hyperion, 1994.

Kelly, Everett. *Everett Kelly's The Atlatl*. College Station, TX: Virtualbookworm. com Publishing Inc., 2004.

Lamme, Bob. *Florida Lore Not Found in the History Books!* Boynton Beach, FL: Star Publishing Company Inc., 1973.

Lapham, Dave. *Ghosthunting Florida.* Cincinnati, OH: Clerisy Press, 2010.

Laumer, Frank. *Massacre!* Gainesville, FL: Rose Printing Company Inc., 1968.

Manaco, C.S. *The Second Seminole War and the Limits of American Aggression.* Baltimore, MD: Johns Hopkins University Press, 2018.

Mayo, Travis M. *The Life and Times of William Henry Mayo: A True Florida Cracker.* USA: Travis M. Mayo Publisher, 2013.

Missall, John, and Mary Lou Missall. *The Seminole Wars: America's Longest Indian Conflict.* Gainesville: University Press of Florida, 2004.

Newton, Michael. *The Encyclopedia of Robberies, Heists, and Capers.* New York: Facts on File Inc., 2002.

Nichols, Hulon H. *Long Hammock Memories.* N.p.: Ideal Publishing Company Inc., 2002.

Parish, Samuel. *Central Florida's Most Notorious Gangsters: Alva Hunt and Hugh Gant.* Charleston, SC: The History Press, 2008.

Sloan, Russ. *Lake & Sumter Counties: "Florida's Heartland."* Dallas, TX: Taylor Specialty Books, 2009.

Smith, Patrick D. *A Land Remembered.* Sarasota, FL: Pineapple Press, 1984.

Villoldo, Alberto, PhD. *Illumination: The Shaman's Way of Healing.* Carlsbad, CA: Hay House Inc., 2010.

Useful Websites

www.airboattoursorlando.com

www.backyardbarnwinery.com

www.bfro.net/GDB/show_county_reports.asp?state=FL&county

www.blog.al.com/live/2013/11/fbi_busts_bonnie_and_clyde-sty.html

www.c1.staticflickr.com/3/2330/1975335192_fa55b9fddb_b.jpg

www.cityofbushnellfl.com

www.communityofroyal.org

www.countyoffice.org

www.dccomics.com/characters/swamp-thing

www.discoversumterfl.com

www.discoversumterfl.com/roosters-on-oxford

www.dos.myflorida.com/florida-facts/florida-history/seminole-history/the-seminole-wars

www.drinklocalflorida.com/wineries-sumter.html

www.fcit.usf.edu/florida/maps/pages/10000/f10055/f10055.htm

www.fcit.usf.edu/florida/maps/pages/3200/f3249/f3249.htm

www.fcit.usf.edu/florida/maps/pages/8600/f8620/f8620.htm

www.fl-genweb.org/sumter/sumcem/nichols.html

www.fl-genweb.org/sumter/sumcem/pine/pinelevelcemintro.html

www.floridamuseum.ufl.edu/flarch/collections

www.floridastateparks.org/parks-and-trails/dade

www.floridazooschool.org

www.gatorworldparks.com/gatorworld-parks-florida

www.hauntedhovel.com/baker-house-wildwood-fl.htm

www.historicalmarkerproject.com/markers/HM25Q2_pilaklikaha-abrahams-town_Center-Hill-FL.htmlPilaklikaha

www.idlewildlodge.com

www.lakeandsumterstyle.com

www.latest-ufo-sightings.net/2016/03/triangle-ufo-sumter

www.legendsofamerica.com/fort-armstrong-florida/

www.loomiscircus.com

www.panavistalodge.com

www.russellstover.com/

www.saundersrealestate.com/property/long-hammock-ranch-in-oxford-florida/

www.schoolplaten.com/afbeelding-ufo-dl26796.jpg

www.seminolehistoricalsociety.org

www.seminolewar.livejournal.com/161207.html

www.spiritanimal.info/turtle-spirit-ani

www.study.com/academy/lesson/florida-cracker-definition-history.html

www.sumterbyway.com

www.sumtercountyfl.gov/235/History-of-Sumter-County

www.sumtercountyhistorical.webs.com

www.sumtercountyhistoricalsociety.org

www.sumtercountymuseum.org

www.sumtercountysheriff.org

www.sumtercountytimes.com

www.sumtertoday.net/towns/Center Hill.htm

www.sun-sentinel.com/news/florida/fl-reg-gator

www.swampfeverairboatadventures.com

www.thevillages.com/thevillageoffenney
www.thevillagesdailysun.com
www.villages1.com
www.waymarking.com
www.websterwestsidefleamarket.com
www.whatismyspiritanimal.com/spirit-totem-power-animal-meanings/
    birds/turtle-symbolism-meaning
www.wildwood-fl.gov
www.winesofflorida.com
www.yelp.com/biz/jailhouse-jeweler-wildwood

About the Author

Gifted from birth as a spiritual medium, mystic, writer and paranormal investigator, Deborah Carr Hollingsworth followed her intuition and heart and now resides deep in the heartland of Florida. She combines her past travel businesses, supernatural experiences and her psychic abilities to find alternate ways to uncover and discover history and haunts.

Prior to her move to Florida, she owned and operated a midwestern historical entertainment company and provided metaphysical workshops, classes, ghost tours and investigations, as well as private psychic readings. Previously, Arcadia Publishing and The History Press released her book *Haunted Bloomington-Normal, Illinois* in 2016 (as Deborah Carr Senger). She has also channeled and portrayed notable women such as Mary Lincoln and Helen Keller, nationally and internationally.

Her recent travels and stops have included Hawaii, Italy, Germany, South Korea, India, the Bahamas, the Carolinas, Missouri, Illinois, Nevada, Indiana, Georgia and Florida.

Deborah's fascination with living history and the spirited dead continues as she explores the backroads and counties in sunny Florida. Her psychic private practice is limited to exclusive personal readings and teaching. Her medium abilities are unleashed supernaturally as she explores all possibilities of bringing and keeping history and haunts alive.

Settled now in the Sunshine State with her husband, Dr. Larry Hollingsworth, and a rescued beagle, Maggie Mae, Deborah continues to enjoy her passionate life on a lake in Fruitland Park.

Contact information for Deborah: spiritsofflorida@gmail.com.